LOVING ADAM

LOVING ADAM

Surviving a Lover with Bipolar Disorder

AMANDA K. HIRSCH

FCP

Full Court Press
Englewood Cliffs, New Jersey

Published in the United States of America
by Full Court Press, 601 Palisade Avenue,
Englewood Cliffs, NJ 07632
fullcourtpressnj.com

All names in this memoir, aside from the author's own, have been changed to protect the identity of those mentioned. In the few cases where a character's real name is used, it is with the express permission of the person being mentioned.

ISBN 978-1-938812-89-7
Library of Congress Catalog No. 2016962950

*Editing and book design by Barry Sheinkopf for Bookshapers
(bookshapers.com)*

To my sister and very best friend, Debbie,
for holding my hand through life every step of the way.

And to my mother, Lucy,
the strongest little woman I know.
You introduced me to God and taught me that, with Faith,
I can accomplish anything.

ACKNOWLEDGMENTS

I'd like to offer a very special thanks to the following people for their support during the events that occurred in this book and the many years it took to make it a reality. You helped me laugh when I wanted to cry, made me brave when I wanted to run, and reminded me I was strong when I felt weak. For this I will be forever grateful.

To my brother-in-law Rob Morgan, an amazing father, brother, and friend. To my nephew Ryan Morgan and niece Olivia, for all the fun and good times. To my niece and god-daughter Casie Morgan, my fellow writer and personal hero, may you learn from my mistakes. To my father Alex R. Hirsch and my brother Alex R. Hirsch, Jr., who were taken from us too quickly. I live my life in tribute to yours.

To my cats Oliver and Lulu—you are my spirit animals, my life force. Your cuddles and snuggles have gotten me through more tough times than I can count. Mommy loves you.

To my Editor, Barry Sheinkopf, for your wisdom and support during this process, and to Eugenia Koukounas, for your friendship and positive light.

To Dr. Wayne Dyer—I never had the honor to meet you, yet I consider you my greatest teacher and eternal friend.

To God—there are no words, only love.

Additional thanks to: Tamarin Hannon (WooWoo), Avia Bushyhead (#SafeToBeMe), Jason Owen, Taro Kawai, Jonathan Hernandez, Anton Za, Tom Marino, Tony Jackson,

Jackie McMann-Oliveri, Dana Abdenour, Jill G. and Anthony R. And to my secret team of muses and angels: Lucinda, Umbita, Euryptes, William, Sam, Gabriel, Aurora, Bixby, Charlie, and Jake

Finally. . .I'd like to thank Adam. It hurt, but it was worth it.

—A.K.H.
San Diego, 2017

PREFACE

❖

THE BLACKBERRY SHOOK FRANTICALLY in my hand. The same number appeared on the screen as on the last nineteen phone calls. It was Adam. I didn't want to answer it, I knew I *shouldn't* answer it, but I did.

"Hooker's in the freezer!" he cried, sobbing between words.

"There's a *hooker* in your freezer?" I asked.

"No!" he wailed. "Hooker, my *cat*. She's in my freezer!"

Oh, my God. Hooker, one of Adam's beloved cats, had been put down a few days before. I was the one who had taken her to the vet when she took a turn for the worse. His ex-wife had told Adam the cat was sick while he was still in the hospital. Somehow he'd gotten himself released to be by Hooker's side when she took her last breath. I could taste his tears through the phone, and in my mind, all I could see was Hooker's tiny, rigid body wedged in his freezer, like a scene from *The Hotel New Hampshire*.

Adam continued his rant. "With all that's going on, the threats on my life and going to the police, I wasn't able to bury her! All I want to do is bury my cat so she doesn't have to be in my freezer." He cried out in pain.

My gut twisted inside. "Adam, do you want me to come pick up the cat and bury her for you?" *Had I really just said that out loud?*

"No!" he yelled, "*I* want to do it! I want *you* to arrange for a car so I can pick up the other kitties tomorrow. Do *not battle* me!"

The kitties he referred to were from the same breeders as Hooker and her sister Cleopatra. He'd reached out to them when he found out Hooker was sick several weeks before. He planned to pick up two new kittens so Cleo had company when Hooker passed. That's what fascinated me about Adam's current state of mind: He'd sounded sane and normal to the breeders when he arranged the sale, but in his mind, he expected me to loan him my mother's car to get what he wanted—the same car I had used to pack up my things when he kicked me out of our apartment in a rage just a few days earlier. I asked him whether he had spoken to Jack, the only therapist he'd ever admitted he trusted with his illness in the past, and the only one he agreed to speak to now. I can't remember how I'd gotten Jack's number, but I had managed to get Adam an appointment. This infuriated him.

"Did you hear me?" His desperation turned to anger. He commanded, "I want you to arrange for the car!"

Calmly I responded, "Adam, you need to confirm your appointment with Jack. It's for 5:15 this evening. You have to call him, and leave a message on his work number that you'll be there."

"I will fucking take care of Jack. You take care of getting me a fucking car!"

"I'll help you get a car *after* I receive word you saw Jack." It was the first condition I set of my own.

". . .What did you say?" His voice rose with the rate of his blood pressure. "What did *you say to me?*"

Uh-oh.

"You fucking whore! You think you can put conditions on *me?*" screamed Adam. "You're *nothing*! You don't get to tell me anything. Fuck you! You will arrange for a car and you'll do it because I'm telling you to do it or I'll have you arrested!"

"Arrest me for what, Adam?" (I knew what was coming.)

"For beating me! That's right! You beat me! I was in pain and you made it worse. I have witnesses! I filed a police report. If you don't do as I say, I'll activate those charges and you will go to *jail!*"

To preserve one of my five treasured senses, I moved the phone away from my ear. Or maybe I just couldn't bear to hear another arrest threat. At that point it broached unoriginal. A few days before Adam's break, he had complained of severe muscular pain in his back and asked me for a massage. He'd said I wasn't going deep enough with my hands and made me stand on him. I had taken it as some type of Geisha-girl, massage-parlor role-play and gone with it. A few days later, when the episode triggered, he had told anyone willing to listen that I'd beaten him. He had promised to file a police report and have me arrested at least four times a day.

"You don't get to order me around anymore, Adam. If you want my help, I'll give it to you, but *not* until I receive word from Jack that you and he met."

"Amanda, if you don't do as I say, *I'll fucking kill you.* I'll take a bus up-state, find you, and blow up your house!"

His anger crossed a new, more violent threshold. "Really, Adam? Now *I'm* calling the police."

"You're a whore!" he shouted. "A fucking home-wrecking whore!"

My head felt dizzy. Minute by minute since the ordeal began, Adam's insults had grown worse, each with more bite than the last.

"You're right, Adam, I'm a home-wrecking whore. But until I get word from Jack that he's seen you, you'll get nothing from me." Frazzled, I hung up the phone.

Rookie mistake. I hadn't yet mastered the rules of the game. I still forgot at times that the man I called Adam was a different man from the one I had fallen in love with two and a half years earlier.

CHAPTER 1

❖

T HE DAY I FIRST LAID EYES on Adam Haddad remains crystal clear in my mind. I had climbed the corporate ladder another rung, and at the start of February 2004, I was set to lead my own personal training department at a gym in New York City. A few days before, I had stopped by to meet the staff and get the lay of the land. As I introduced myself to the general manager, Adam had appeared from one of the offices. My head had tilted slightly to the side, the way a dog tilts its head when intrigued. There was something *familiar* about him. His dark brown eyes and thick, long eyelashes reminded me of my mother's side of our family. I figured that must be it. Then I felt creepy for tilting my head in that way towards someone who reminded me of my cousins.

When I finally began my new role, I learned Adam was engaged to marry a lovely girl named Beth in September. She was a personal trainer for another gym franchise, simultaneously pursuing an opera career. She was intelligent, cultured, and attractive enough to imagine she made Adam happy. She often visited him at the gym to say hello or have lunch. They sat side by side when they ate at his desk, and showed discreet displays of affection around the rest of us.

Our work team was like a family, and as such, we got to know one another's spouses and significant others fairly well. On several occasions, we all went out together, but unlike Adam, Beth didn't love to socialize. Most nights she politely sat off to the side while Adam danced and played with the rest of us. Then she cried too much to drink and asked to leave early. We all saw the differences in their personalities, but Beth seemed to keep Adam in line, and publicly they appeared happy. Back then I was still in a relationship with my ex, Sean. For all intents and purposes, Adam was off limits, not an option. That September, he and Beth married.

Over the course of the next two years, Adam and I grew to be close friends, with an uncommon tendency to hate each other on occasion. The gym business produced a high-pressure, long-hours environment where we all worked towards a common goal. We formed a precious bond with our fellow co-workers one doesn't often encounter professionally. Adam and I were both smokers, and through several quick breaks a day, our dynamic evolved. Over time we discovered each other's strengths and weaknesses: I his strengths, and he my weaknesses. I told him everything without concern at some point it might come back to haunt me. Adam was highly skilled at revealing the parts of him guaranteed to draw others in. (*Lesson learned.*)

We shared a common interest in pot. I am a full supporter of the legalization of marijuana, but I won't get political about it now. This common thread connected us in a different way than he was able to with Beth, as did much of our conversation and interests. Add to that whatever issues they had at home, and some version of disaster was set to brew long before I had anything to do with it. Both Adam and I were in our late twenties and struggled with the growing pains of adulthood, each of us impressed with the other's progress. Beth had severe control issues and I saw Adam bend over backwards to satisfy her. He once made Beth show me a weekly calendar she kept of all the times Adam smoked pot and who he smoked with. At the time I found it tenderly obsessive. I couldn't imagine keeping tabs on someone that way, let alone someone like Adam who was in all ways a Leo that wouldn't be controlled. To this day, I still feel Beth had the best of Adam. It sounds ridiculous considering how things turned out, but part of why I fell for him was because of certain ways I witnessed him love Beth. It sounds cliché, but clichés are clichés for a reason.

By December 2005, I lost close to forty pounds and found a sexy new confidence. The general-manager position at my gym location opened up, and I was offered the chance to take over. Now I was Adam's boss. Up until then I had viewed him as an annoying (married) brother who pushed my buttons in a playful way, but he ended up surprisingly supportive during my promotion. For the first time I started to think that, if Beth had not been in the picture, Adam and I might have had a chance.

It was a subtle transition from "co-workers" to "friends" to "something more." Subtle meaning: I had no real clue it was happening. As much as I'd like to model myself with the confidence of Angelina Jolie in any of her movies, I don't always recognize when someone has feelings for me, especially when that someone is married. Still, the signs were there.

While at work, we spent all the time we could together. There was a secret spot within the building a few of us would go to sneak a cigarette or pass around a one-hitter for a jolt of herbal, afternoon, refreshment. It was sneaky, inappropriate and oh-so-much fun. One day after his workout, I received a text from Adam that read: *Adam: Cum upstairs.*

Sure I noticed the spelling of *come*, but in a world with a new shorthand called text, I LOL'd it away. Later that night, my phone rang with Adam's number on the caller ID. Outside of work, we were not phone friends. Sheer curiosity prompted me to answer.

"Hello?"

"Oh, hi? Who's this?" said Adam's wife, Beth.

"Beth? It's Amanda from the gym."

"Oh, hi!" said Beth. "I'm sorry, I accidentally took Adam's phone and must've dialed your number by accident."

That's a little too many accidents if you ask me. I told her it was no big deal and continued with small talk. She was pleasant and joked about her absentmindedness. It wasn't until some time later I realized Beth's call was an attempt to dig deeper into Adam's Freudian text. She sensed there was something between Adam and I long before I did.

My last clear vision of Adam and Beth as a happy couple happened one evening in late March 2006. They joined a few of us from work for dinner and drinks at a nearby Cuban restaurant. They were the first to arrive, Adam had ordered an appetizer and we met them at the bar while we all waited for our table. Suddenly, Adam offered me a bite of his food and before I could answer, he leaned in and fed me a forkful, as Beth watched.

You may read this and think, *Who cares?* You may gasp. In my head, as I swallowed, *I* gasped. No woman I knew ever wanted her man to feed another woman, but I couldn't imagine Adam being that dumb on purpose. I figured he knew Beth was secure with our friendship and wouldn't mind. *(Yeah, right.)*

Say what you want about Adam, he's extremely physically attractive. He's one of those men with an ultra-high metabolism that spends his life at four percent body fat no matter what he eats. Working out is an essential part of his daily routine and when he's on track eating enough, his body responds tremendously. At his worst he compares to Brad Pitt in *Fight Club*, a smaller frame but extremely defined. At his best he's statuesque. It's quite frustrating, really.

Shortly after we received our main course, one of the girls asked Beth if she was excited about how muscular Adam had gotten and how good he looked. Beth seemed startled by the question.

"Yes, the other night Adam sat on the couch in a tank top, and I thought to myself, *He looks good.*" Her tone sounded genuinely surprised.

I smiled and thought, *If I had Adam on my couch in a tank top, I'd fuckin' rip it off him.* I found it sad Beth didn't put it that way.

After dinner, the others and I went to a bar for more fun while the married couple chose to head home. Before they walked off hand-in-hand, they exchanged a soft, simple kiss that made us all "*Awww*" in unison. I sat in the back of the cab as we pulled away and listened to the girls who worked for me blabber on about how cute they were. Okay, okay, I admit it—they fooled me too, but before long, the truth became clear.

A few days later, I sat at my computer behind the front desk fixated on work. Adam interrupted me with some conversation.

"Burning Spear is playing tonight at Irving Place." Adam loved reggae.

Focused on my screen, I responded, "Oh, yeah? That's cool."

"Beth doesn't want to go. I'm gonna go anyway."

"Have fun." I replied at half attention. He left for a few moments and returned with his iPod.

"Here, listen to this."

Suddenly I felt his fingers place something in my ears and heard some very smooth, chill tunes I couldn't help but sway to.

"This is Burning Spear?" I asked.

"Yeah, you like him?"

"Sure, he sounds good." I removed the ear buds and went back to typing.

"He's really great live. These reggae concerts are awesome. Everyone smokes up like it's legal. The cops don't bother you. You should go."

"Sounds fun."

"You should go," he repeated.

Then it hit me. "Adam, are you asking me to go with you to the concert, so you don't have to go alone?"

"Sure, you want to?" His eyes lit up.

"Well. . . ."

"Come on, let's go! Let's go get tickets now."

Before I knew it, he pulled out my chair and ushered me out of the gym towards Irving Plaza. His little plan was set in motion. Soon we'd be blazing at a reggae concert together, dancing and who knew what else. To Adam's dismay, I called my buddy Mike on my cell to see if he wanted to tag along. The more, the merrier I thought, and just like that, Adam's duo became a crowd.

A crowd, yes, but not for long. The three of us arrived at the concert that evening and quickly got drinks. Adam wasn't lying when he said people smoked at these events. Clouds of Mary Jane filled the air and everyone got along. As the lights flickered, Adam nudged me to the front of the venue, center stage. The crowd filled up behind us. The stage grew dark, then colorful with lights. An African American man with white hair and vibrant clothing came out to perform. He appeared in his sixties but sang with the energy and passion of a man decades younger.

The whole crowd danced, entranced by sound and smoke. I suddenly felt a man come up behind me, place his hands on my waist, and move with me in rhythm to the island beats. It was Adam. He felt so good and fit so perfectly it surprised me. We continued to dance the entire night. I imagine Mike felt like a third wheel. We lost track of him after the first couple of songs. Despite how good it felt with Adam, I still thought it was innocent. Like dancing with a gay man; anything more was simply not an option. I even considered Beth lucky to know her husband was out with me. *Someone she could trust.*

None of us knew that one dance with Adam would lead to the rest.

We had never anticipated the strength of our attraction once our bodies finally touched. Beth had no idea if she skipped one concert, it would change the rest of her life, but it did. The next day, a friend asked me how the concert had gone. I told her I'd danced with Adam and said, "If only he were single. . . ." To my surprise, it turned out in the end, that wasn't what mattered most.

CHAPTER 2

❖

FTER THE CONCERT, THINGS CHANGED between Adam and me. We began to look at each other differently and we both silently noticed it in the other. We found more and more excuses to spend time together during the workday. With no office of my own, I had plenty of reason and opportunity to share with him.

One evening, as we both gathered our things to go our separate ways for the day, Adam walked me out the door and convinced me to go for a drink with him at Coffee Shop, just a few blocks away. We never really went out alone before, and for the first time I felt a shadow of the Devil on my shoulder warning of what could happen. Still. . . *it was only a shadow*.

We found seats in the back of the restaurant among the crowd at the bar. Two Mojitos later, we discussed everything under the sun from religion to politics to our family dramas. Even I couldn't deny it was our first date. My blissful ignorance of how Adam felt about me quickly dissipated. Adam eventually stated it was getting late and we should head to my place to smoke before he had to go home. The Devil's shadow grew darker, but I agreed nonetheless.

We cabbed it to my tiny, overpriced studio apartment where I lived with my two cats, Oliver and Lulu, at the corner of Bleecker Street and

Sixth Avenue. The main room couldn't fit more than my bed and a small chair. Adam chose to sit at the end of the bed; I sat across from him in the chair. He rolled a blunt for us to share as I stared out the fire escape window, with nothing but our reflection staring back at me. After a few minutes, our steady conversation grew quiet.

"I need to ask you something," said Adam.

I sensed his question without a word. "Don't, Adam."

"You don't know what I want to ask you," he spoke softly, his voice full of nerves.

"Yes, I do. And I don't think you should—"

"I want to kiss you."

My heart raced.

". . .May I kiss you?" he seductively pleaded.

I gave an ethical response, but my tone lacked conviction: "I don't think it's a good idea."

"Please. I've wanted this for a long time. I need to get it out of my system," he said.

I had literally heard those words before, and way too often. Over the years many of my unavailable male friends had approached me with the same request. It was a pattern I wasn't proud of. My internal warning system approached Defcon 3 while the Devil on my shoulder dusted off his fiddle.

"But what if you *don't* get it out of your system?" I asked.

"I will," replied Adam. "Just this one night. I've wanted you for months now, and it's all I think about. I just need to get it out of my system. No sex. Just a kiss. . . . *Please.*"

When I was a kid, I read this series of books called *Choose Your Own Adventure*. It was a story like any other, but at different points it offered you the chance to choose the next step. *If you want Bobby to go into the haunted house, turn to page 45. If you want Bobby to go back to the baseball field, turn to page 67.* I wish I could do the same for you now. I wish it were as easy as saying,

If you'd like Amanda to kindly ask Adam to leave, turn to page 35. However, if you prefer to witness the power of what any single choice can yield. . .keep reading.

The Devil played my tune. I was single, and I had Adam right in front of me, begging to give me the chance to feel something I couldn't help but want to feel. I'd like to say my mind went blank and I blacked out. *Not guilty by reason of temporary insanity*. But I can't. I had a choice. I played this game before. And what's worse? I knew Beth. I *liked* Beth! Yet here I was, guilty as sin of wanting to taste her husband's lips, and better yet, those lips urging me to do so. *'Just this one night...'* he said. In that moment, all that mattered was the moment. I had a million reasons to say no, but only one reason to say yes: *A chance to really live.* I didn't want to wonder about Adam anymore, I wanted to *know*. Adam didn't wait for me to answer. He leaned in, grazed my cheek with his hand, and then it happened.

The inevitable fireworks used to describe a kiss, long before Katy Perry made the song famous. When our lips first touched, we pulled back startled by what we felt. When they touched again, we knew it was no illusion. We fit perfectly together. We *kissed* perfectly together. It was more than foreplay or sensory fulfillment. It was *magic*. When we finally came up for air, we knew there was no turning back. Within moments, *No sex, just a kiss* had been transformed into *No sex. . .but please consume me in whatever way possible.*

Adam pulled me close to him, laid me down on the bed, and got on top of me. My legs quickly wrapped around him. His hand cradled my head, and he kissed me with a gentle passion, as though I were a treasured Fabergé egg. He stopped briefly to gaze in my eyes, both of us entranced by our connection. I touched my hand to his face to make sure I wasn't dreaming and slowly traced his sculpted arms with my fingers. He kissed me again.

It was like diving into a cold pool during a heat wave: An intense shock and awe of euphoria entangled my body and numbed me to consequence. Adam's tongue synchronized with mine, pausing just enough to taste my skin, kiss my neck. His hand slid down my torso, and I felt him beneath my shirt. I moaned as his fingers caressed my stomach, traveled upwards over my bra, and guided the strap off my shoulder. At the same time, his other hand reached around my back and, with one flick, he engulfed my bare breasts, my nipples rigid with desire.

"Who are you, Fonzie?" I teased him.

Adam smiled. His gorgeous dimples hypnotized me. He pushed my shirt up slightly and powdered my belly with tender kisses.

"So soft," he whispered.

His mouth moved towards the waist of my pants.

Oh, God, I thought. *Is he gonna. . . ? I think he might—*

He unbuttoned my jeans and slid down my zipper.

"Adam—I don't know. . .I'm not sure—"

"Shh. It's just tonight. *No sex.*"

It's just tonight, I thought. Here I was with a man I fantasized about on several occasions, and reality exceeded any fantasy I imagined. Now he wanted to pleasure me, and what's more, took great pleasure in doing so.

"Okay." I conceded and prepared for rapture.

Adam returned his lips to my body, both hands gripped to the sides of my jeans. Between my legs I felt damp in anticipation of his arrival. His tongue tickled the curves of my hips and moved towards my inner thigh. With one hand, Adam pulled my pants to the floor; his other took hold of my V-String. I trembled with anxious excitement. Suddenly I felt the rush of his warm tongue, the heat from his breath and his fingers play me like Mozart.

"*Oh. . .my. . .God,*" I moaned softly, growing louder the more he moved. In my head I recalled all the sexual conversations we previously shared as friends. Inadvertently admitting what we liked and how we like it done. Either Adam took notes when I spoke, or he's been blessed with a rare super-power: *G-Spot Vision*. My body quivered and jumped with each thrust and swish of his mouth. He released a steady, mild hum sending hot pulses to my senses like a human vibrator.

I opened my eyes to watch him and witness the ecstasy that consumed me. Never much a fan of erotic art, I couldn't help but wish I had a camera. I marveled at the beauty of him below my waist, dedicated to my extreme satisfaction.

"God, you taste so good," he whispered.

With that, I sat up, took hold of his tank top and ripped it over his head the way I always wanted to. He resembled David, each muscle visible through lines crafted by some ancient God. A faint 'wow' escaped as I exhaled that made Adam pause and pull me close, into a deep kiss. I tasted the mixture of us on his breath and craved him more. I put my mouth to his ear and quietly spoke, "*My turn.*"

Adam's eyes widened and for a moment I thought he looked scared. I giggled as I repositioned myself on top of him, all the while nuzzling his neck. He purred like a cat. If this was my one chance at Adam, I was going to savor every second of it.

As a fitness expert, I'm an aficionado of the human body. As a woman, I'm a particular fan of the male body, and as Amanda, I was the biggest fan of Adam's. I pulled away from him to get a good look. Soft, smooth skin with the perfect amount of man-hair in all the right places. I worked my way down his torso sampling each section like a fine wine; my lips rose and fell between each toned abdominal square. Washboards should pay this man homage.

My mouth reached his waist and I felt Adam shake. I looked up at him as I unbuttoned his pants, feeling him hard through his boxers. His skin peaked through the fabric opening and I grazed it first with my hands, then my lips. I looked up at him again, seductively, as I took him in my mouth.

"Ho-ly *shit!*" he shouted.

While I may consider myself to be a very sexual person, don't confuse that with me being a slut. My sexual encounters can all be accounted for and most of them happened with someone who mattered significantly to me. Sex is a key ingredient to maintaining a monogamous relationship, and when I'm in a monogamous relationship, I do what I can to keep the fire alive for as long as possible. Turns out a good way for women to bond sexually with their men is quite simple: Bond with the penis.

We all know men have two heads and the smaller of the two is in charge. The best way to bond with the penis is through blow jobs. I know many women don't like to give them and if I could give one piece of advice it's get over it. Men *love* blow jobs and men love their penis. Men love women who love both blow jobs and their penis. *You* do the math.

Adam was well aware of my 'bond with your man through his penis' theory. If this was our one and only night together, he was (for damn sure) going to remember it.

I closed my eyes and took him in my mouth. The rest of his body went limp and his lips pursed a sound of sheer joy. The more he moaned, the more I took him in, sliding gently up and down his shaft, tickling his tip with my tongue. My hands explored the rest of his body, gripping him tightly from underneath his legs, pulling him further down my throat, devoted to making him cum. His penis was beautiful like the rest of him, just the right size and shape. For a moment I felt like a porn version of Goldilocks and I had to admit, I wanted this bear's porridge. A few minutes later. . .that too was just right.

Exhausted, I rest my head on Adam's stomach and he reached down for my arms, pulling me close to his chest. It was the first moment I realized the room was silent. We hadn't put on any music or turned on the TV. We had been engrossed in each other, making our own joyful noise.

"It was better than I ever imagined," whispered Adam.

"I know," I said. "Unbelievable how well we fit together."

The chime of a bell pierced the quiet air and a text message from Beth burst the bubble we had temporarily built around us. Our night had come to a close. We were back in reality.

"I had a great time with you tonight," said Adam as I walked him to the door.

"Me, too. It was fun."

He grew quiet for a moment and hugged me close to him. He smelled my hair and sighed. "I didn't know it would feel this good."

"Well," I joked, "I warned ya."

He kissed me again. A piece of me never wanted to let go.

He whispered, "Thank you for a wonderful evening."

Intoxicated by 'one night' with Adam I said goodbye with a grin on my face, unwittingly primed to play his fool.

CHAPTER 3

❖

T HE NEXT MORNING, Adam greeted me with a smile as I walked past his desk. "Good morning," I said glad to get the awkwardness over with. After taking an extra few seconds to breathe while stowing my bag and coat, I closed the door to find Adam standing behind me. He smelled delicious.

"Ready for breakfast?" he asked.

We had a ritual. Each morning we went to the deli on the corner, ordered breakfast and took our coffees outside as we smoked a cigarette and waited for our food. Then we ate together in Adam's office. To disrupt the routine would imply things had changed between us. Since I wouldn't yet admit that to myself, I chose to play it cool and hope Adam would let sleeping dogs lie.

"Sure, let's go." I grabbed my bag from the closet and off we went.

A thick silence lingered between us like an eight-hundred-pound gorilla. After we placed our orders and made our way outside to wait, Adam finally spoke.

"I, uh. . .had a good time last night."

So much for sleeping dogs. I took a sip of my coffee and a long pull from my cigarette to stall for a response.

"Me, too." My face grew flushed and warm. Adam smiled at my shyness and I giggled like a schoolgirl. "I had a very good time."

"I knew we'd be good together," he said. Just not *that* good."

"I know," I answered. "It was a pleasant surprise."

Adam's face grew serious. "I just want you to know. . .I don't do this."

"Do what?" I asked.

"This. I mean. . .*cheat*. I don't want you to think I do this all the time or I'm that kind of guy. I've never done this before. It's just that. . .well, it was *you*." His eyes shifted away. "Things haven't been very good at home with Beth for a while now."

I knew the tale all too well. Adam wasn't the first unavailable man to confess feelings for me. I stopped him. "Adam, you don't have to explain it to me but I'll say this much—you and Beth hide your troubles well."

"Yes," he said. "We do our best to hide it in public."

"Well—" I tossed my cigarette butte to the ground— "as they say in *When Harry Met Sally*: *Marriages don't break up on account of infidelity. It's just a symptom that something else is wrong.* Whatever you two are going through, I'm sure you'll work it out."

He looked at me as if he wished I were a doll he could carry around in his pocket. Instinctively, I turned away.

"I know we'll work it out," he went on. "But we've been married for nineteen months now, and I can count the number of times we've had sex on both hands."

"Ouch!" I said. "*Why?*"

He struggled with the answer. "I'm not... I'm not attracted to her like that. She's a wonderful person and I owe her a lot, but she has this . . .*odor*—"

"Oh, God, stop." I didn't want to know.

"And she's very *hairy*."

| 20 |

"Adam, don't!" The thought grossed me out. Or, the guilt gave me an ulcer. I wasn't sure which.

"I'm sorry!" he laughed. "I'm not trying to be mean, I'm trying to make you understand why this happened between us."

"Well didn't you know this when you married her?"

"I thought it would pass," he said. "She did so much for me. I thought I could deal with it. I *was* dealing with it. Until. . .you."

"Why me?" I asked, half to him and half to the Universe.

He didn't hesitate. "Because you're wonderful!"

(My heart went pitter.)

"And you're beautiful."

(My heart went patter.)

"And I'm completely attracted to everything about you, every part of you. My God, when we kissed. . . . When I *tasted* you—"

"Okay, okay. Enough."

He kept talking as he opened the door to the deli to retrieve our food. "I *can't* go down on her. I just can't. I feel bad, but the few times I have, I had to stop, I almost threw up."

"Jesus, Adam. That's not good."

"I've been thinking about you for so long now. I think about you when I'm with her. I jerk off to you when I'm in the shower!"

"*Adam!*" I smacked his arm and scanned the immediate area for eavesdroppers. He enjoyed making me blush.

"I'm sorry, but it's true," said Adam.

"Look, I'll admit I wondered about you, too." He looked proud. "But trust me, you and Beth will work things out. Right now you're just confused about what's going on at home, and it's not like what happened last night is ever gonna happen again."

"Right," Adam agreed. "Although, I could come by again tonight."

"No, Adam."

"To give you a massage?"

"Are you crazy?" I snapped at him. "We said only one time!"

"You wouldn't even have to touch me. I just want to give you a massage and worship you the way you deserve. You're a goddess."

I may have been his goddess, but the Devil had now bought a timeshare in my soul. I saw a flash of Adam's hands on my back and suddenly forgot where I was until I heard a man shout our food was ready.

"So tonight, then?" Asked Adam. "I'll bring some wine."

"Food's ready," I answered.

For the remainder of the day, we met eyes whenever we could. Each time Adam had me alone, he referenced the night before in some spectacular way, as though being with me was a gift too grand to fathom. I couldn't remember the last time a man made me feel that way (or if any man ever had). He found any reason he could to touch me. Once he removed an eyelash from my face then later, a piece of thread from my sleeve. The closer he stood to me, the more electricity raced between us.

During my workout, Adam approached my treadmill and asked me to share a smoke with him at our secret spot in the outdoor, stairwell corridors. As soon as we cleared the corner where we knew we couldn't be seen, we grabbed each other in a fiery kiss, like we were the only drug or vice the other needed.

"So. . .*tonight?*" whispered Adam as he held me against his chest. "One massage. I promise. I want to make you feel good and use my hands to memorize your body."

I caved. This man, his kiss, and his hands on my body usurped my ethical mind. "You know I warned you about this, right?"

"Warned me about what?" he asked.

"That you might not get me *out of your system.*"

"Oh, *that.*" He smiled and kissed me softly. He stroked my face. "Turns out you were right."

That evening, he left a few minutes before me to avoid suspicion. I managed to beat him to my apartment and prepared for his arrival. My hands shook and my heart fluttered when the buzzer rang. We said hello through a passionate kiss the moment I opened the door. Each kiss made me grow dangerously closer to him, but still I didn't pull away.

"Just in case I don't get another chance," said Adam.

There, seated in the same spots as the night before when everything changed between us, we smoked and drank in our own personal world. One night had become two, but we embraced each moment as though it our last. As a spurt of our laughter died down, Adam told me it was time and asked me to stand.

"Time for what?" I asked.

He smiled coyly and went to the corner to get something from his bag. He returned with a selection of oils and lotions. "Your massage."

I looked at his tools. "And you just happen to carry these around with you?"

He laughed. "No, gorgeous. I stopped at Pleasure Chest on the way here."

"Adam, this isn't a good idea. None of this is a good idea."

"Please, Amanda. Let me do this to you—I mean, *for* you. Let me do this *for you*."

"But—"

"But nothing. You work so hard every day," said Adam. "I see you with the members and what you go through. *Please.* Let me make you feel good. Let me feel your body with my hands so I can remember you fully when I'm not with you. I'm an artist, I have an appreciation for the female form. Right now, more specifically, your female form."

We stood in the center of my cramped apartment and when I attempted to speak, nothing came out. I gazed into his stunning brown eyes and replayed his last few words in my head. For the first time in a long time, I felt truly wanted by a man, utterly desired. I meant to say no, but when I tried, the words failed me.

Adam took his queue from my lack of effort to stop him. He held my face tenderly, then gently traced the length of my arms as they hung at my side. He raised my arms up over my head and pulled off my t-shirt. He turned me away from him, tickled me with his fingertips down the length of my back and moved towards my stomach to unbutton my jeans. I felt faint. His hands tugged on the denim and he lowered my pants to the floor, slowly freeing one leg at a time from the crumpled fabric.

He ascended again with care, and traced the length of my body with his soft lips. He kissed my waist, my shoulders, and finished at my neck. He unsnapped my bra, but didn't remove it. I felt his warm breath against my ear as his hand slid beneath the front fabric of my underwear. A blissful sigh escaped me.

"Lie down," he whispered.

My chemistry with Adam set off my inner sexy, and the more I turned him on, the easier it was to access. I seductively moved to the bed, sure to accentuate the curves I knew mattered to him. Soon, drops of oil fell against my skin and Adam's hands gripped my body. To say it felt good would be an injustice. He took his time and relished every inch of me. Adam proved again that whatever he did, he did well. After at least an hour of relaxing and comfortable silence, he asked, "So how do you feel?"

"Grateful." I gingerly sat up, placed my bra around Adam's neck and pulled him close for a kiss. "Let me show you how *grateful* I am." Our bodies merged and before long, we were at it again, determined to consume all we could of each other, while maintaining the rule of *No sex*.

At the end of the night, I walked Adam to the door, thankful no text-bells had rung during what was sure to be our last tryst.

"I'm *really* glad we had tonight," said Adam as he hugged me tightly goodbye.

"Me, too. It's fair to say if all else fails, you'd make one hell of a massage therapist."

He looked genuinely rewarded by my satisfaction. "You enjoyed it?"

"Best massage of my life," I smiled.

This made him kiss me. Before pulling away, he pressed his head gently to mine. We lingered for a moment, entangled in some spiritual connection neither of us could deny, nor would we acknowledge for fear of the complications that would ensue.

Without moving I mumbled, "This has to stop, you know."

Adam sighed heavily. "I know."

"It's not fair to Beth," I said. "She's a good woman and she doesn't deserve this."

"I know," he agreed. "It's not fair that I feel this way about you. It's not fair that it feels this good to be with you. I never felt like this before, I didn't know it could be like this. If I had known, I never– " He paused before he said anything he might regret.

"Let's simply be grateful for what little we did have, and stop things now before they get out of hand. Right or wrong, I'll never regret kissing you," I told him.

Adam squeezed me tightly one last time. He took both my hands in his and kissed each fingertip. "Thank you, Amanda. *For everything*."

"Thank you, Adam. *Goodnight*." I closed the door to my apartment and took pause to process the last forty-eight hours.

CHAPTER 4

❖

A ND SO BEGAN A TIME IN MY LIFE I never imagined would happen. Adam and I made minimal attempts to put things behind us. Over the course of the next few weeks, I pursued other dating opportunities, while Beth became more of a presence around the gym. Yet in between, Adam and I grew closer. Our smoke breaks continued and so did our conversations. Each one taught us more about the other.

As they say, hindsight is 20/20. All those years ago, my mind was in a different place when things started with Adam. My priorities at the time, highly confused. A single girl with a demanding career and severe Daddy issues. After a childhood spent watching TV and film I was definitely too young for, drama fueled my fantasies in adulthood, and I often let it frame my reality. My level of sexual attraction to someone determined the extent we were "meant to be" and with Adam, the floodgate was opened. I trusted people blindly, believing them always good before bad. I wore my heart on my sleeve and often got hurt in the process. Adam would say he loved these things about me. He wanted to be the guy to change it all. He had insider access to my soul and made me feel like someone saw the real me. . .*and loved her*.

One day, we sat on the red staircase next door to the gym for one of our five-minute breaks as I filled him in on a date I had the night before.

"So did you let him kiss you goodnight?" asked Adam. His head hung low.

"Yes, I did."

"And?"

"And *what*?" I asked.

"Did you enjoy it?"

"It was okay, I guess."

Adam sighed in relief. "Just okay?"

"Yup."

"What went wrong?" He prodded.

"He was sloppy," I said. "Like a wet machine gun in my mouth, darting in and out."

"Gross!" he laughed. "So it wasn't like with us?"

Surprised he had to ask I replied, "No. Not like with us."

Adam grinned. "What do you like about us when we kiss?" He acted like a schoolboy who sought praise for his skills.

"Well... I love how you touch my face when we kiss. You use your lips just as much as your tongue and at just the right times."

He nodded. "Thanks. I learned from years of watching *General Hospital* with my grandma when I was a kid."

"*General Hospital?* I love that show! You watched it with your grandmother?"

"I still do if I'm home and it's on."

"No, you don't! You're just saying that because you know I watch it. Stop trying to get into my pants," I teased.

"Ha! I swear. I know all the characters!" said Adam. "Luke, Laura. . .Sonny and Brenda. . . . Remember when Sonny and Brenda got shot at in Puerto Rico?"

We exchanged memorable plot lines for a bit and inside I cursed the Gods for giving me another reason to find Adam adorable.

Adam held the door for me as we returned to the gym. When we approached his office, I instinctively followed him in and sat down. He proceeded to bang away on the keyboard and I answered emails via my phone.

After a few minutes Adam broke the silence. "Can I ask you something?"

"You can ask me anything, Adam."

"Next weekend, Beth is leaving to visit her mom up north. I was wondering if we could spend the week together?"

He stunned me. Surely he knew I meant anything except that.

"Or I could stay with you?" he asked again.

Despite my lust for him physically, it was how much I grew to like Adam's personality that cautioned my defenses. "I don't think so, Adam. It wouldn't be a smart thing to do."

"Come on," he pleaded. "We could sleep next to each other every night and wake up together every morning. We could go to work together, leave together. It would be like we were a real couple!"

"For a week," I added. "And we'll probably love it and it will be that much harder when it ends."

"But we'll always have that week. Please Amanda, I want to know what it's like to hold you in my arms as I fall asleep."

"I'm sorry, Adam. You won't be the one who ends up hurt in this equation."

"We're both already hurting being apart," he countered.

"Exactly my point," I said. "It will only get worse if we let it keep getting better. Plus what about Beth? Here she's trusting you and you're planning an affair."

"Alright stop." Adam went back to his computer. "Forget I said it."

"Good idea."

After thirty seconds of latent, angry quiet, the front desk rang to tell him he had a prospect. Before I opened the door to go he stopped me. With soft, desperate eyes he asked again.

"Think about it, Amanda? . . . Please?"

"Fine," I said. "I'll *think* about it."

CHAPTER 5

❖

TIME HAS ALWAYS FASCINATED ME. The way some weeks go by
like days, and others have the impact of a thousand years. Too
often it's happened that I wake up in the morning and go to bed
a drastically different person from events transpired over the course of
a few hours. Ever get the phone call a loved one has passed? Ever get
offered a new job? These are fleeting moments that can change the
course of a lifetime. When powerful emotions such as lust and love
come together, time becomes irrelevant. Seconds are savored and days
move at the speed of light. When all is said and done, you're never the
same.

Beth left on a Friday and planned to return the following weekend.
Neither of us meant to hurt her, but Adam and I agreed for one week
to let it be about us and set misgivings aside. The threat of Beth seeing
us was gone for a little while, but we still needed to use caution when in
public. Of all the nearby areas, my neighborhood in the West Village
posed the least threat of exposure. We started the week with dinner at
an Ethiopian restaurant on MacDougal Street, around the corner from
my apartment. The restaurant was virtually empty, but we took a table
in the back just in case.

Adam took my hand from across the table. "It's our first date!"

"It sure is," I replied.

The waiter brought us our menus. More of a cheeseburger and fries gal, my face read fear when I saw words like *Doro Wat* and *Miser Alech* as my meal choices. So much so it made Adam laugh.

"You okay there?" he asked.

I looked at him. "I have no idea what any of this is."

"It's okay," he said. "I'll order for both of us. You've never eaten Ethiopian food before?"

"I'm not much of a foodie."

"Well that's why we're here. To get you out of the gym and trying new things." He leaned in and kissed me tenderly.

There it was. *Attractive quality number one: Worldly, adventurous, willing to try new things.* I was a sucker for men with this quality. Knowledge is sexy as hell and having spent most days as a decision maker, I welcomed the chance for someone to lead the way.

Our dinner arrived and we talked as we ate. As close as I had become with Adam, there was still so much I didn't know. Many of the stories about his past or ambitions for his future I heard third hand from other coworkers. Now was my chance to hear them straight from him.

"So you grew up an artist?" I asked.

"Yes, I did." He took a bite of his food.

"How old were you when you first knew you could draw?"

"My Grandma gave me my first issue of *Playboy* when I was five. The *Madonna* issue!" laughed Adam.

I almost spit out my food. "Your *grandma* gave it to you?"

"Yeah. She saw I had some skill and gave me the magazine so I could practice figure drawing the naked women."

"At *five*?" I shrieked.

"Yeah. My friends were all jealous."

"Wow," I said. "Now it all makes sense."

"Ha! What does?" asked Adam.

"*You!* You're love of boobs, women and strip clubs. It's your grandma's fault!"

Adam chuckled. "Let's just say I'm *very good* at sketching the female form."

"Your mom didn't mind?"

"Mind? Are you kidding? I'm an only child. I could do no wrong."

"That explains so much," I teased.

"Explains what exactly?" asked Adam.

"Why you never stop anything until you get what you want."

Adam smiled as I hit the nail on the head. "That's how you succeed. It's all part of the process."

"Process?" I asked.

"Yes, the process of getting what you want. You can never give up. My art is a perfect example."

"How?"

"I spent my childhood learning technique and honing my craft. I went to the New World School of Arts in Miami for high school, specifically for visual arts. It's prestigious for that sort of thing."

"Is that how you met the President?" I asked.

"Yeah. One of my paintings won the White House Commission of Presidential Scholars for Visual Art in 1996. I got to attend a ceremony where I met Bill Clinton."

"That's amazing!" I said in awe. "What was the painting of?"

"My grandmother, Ruth, just before she died from cancer. It was actually a huge project, not just paint. I put photos of my mom and I in it, different flowers and leaves, I even have some of Grandma Ruth's ashes in the painting."

"My God, it sounds beautiful."

"I took care of my grandma when she was sick." Adam's voice cracked with emotion as he cut his food. "I would go to school and then go see her everyday in the hospital. I managed to maintain straight A's, too."

"What about your mom?"

"My mom?" Adam snickered under his breath, "Let's just say I was more like a parent to my mother than she was to me. My grandmother really raised me."

"I'm sorry," I said, my hand reaching for his in empathy. My mother is the definition of a great mom, like one of God's angels walking among us. The idea of anything less seemed incomprehensible.

Adam's eyes glistened. "Ruth passed away when I was 17. On her death bed I promised her I would always take care of my mother."

"That's a lot of responsibility to take on yourself."

"Well, that's been the way of it most of my life. When I was five, my father came to me and asked me if I wanted him to stay with us. He said if I wanted him to, he'd put whatever feelings for my mother aside and stay. I just had to say the word."

"My God, what did you say?"

"I told him to leave," said Adam.

"You *did?* I didn't think a toddler could even understand that type of situation."

"Yeah, even as a boy I knew they wouldn't work out. My mother's a Jew, my father is from Iran: It was doomed from the start." Adam joked.

"No wonder your grandma bought you porn," I replied.

"Honestly though, I'm the neutral ground between the two enemy cultures of my parents. I love it! It's helped me all my life."

"Helped you how?" I wondered.

"Understanding how each side thinks allows me to work with both sides from their own perspective, all the while earning trust from each culture as one of their people. One day I will find a way to bridge the gap between Jews and Muslims on a large scale."

"So your ultimate goal is world peace?" I confirmed.

Adam clinked my glass. "Ya gotta think big to be big, gorgeous."

Attractive quality, number two: Ambitious, goal-oriented winner; masterpiece artist, on quest for world peace.

Adam held the door again for me as we left. The street was busy with weekend nightlife and for the first time, Adam's fingers locked with mine as we walked. It felt natural being with him. He put me at ease. We stopped at a nearby café for dessert and brought it back to my apartment. We weren't drunk or stoned, or desperate for one chance with the other. We were calm, at peace and eager to enjoy each other's company. Something was changing between us. The more time we spent together the more it wasn't just Adam's body I wanted. It was his mind and heart as well. That night, when I finally laid my head against Adam's chest and kissed him goodnight, I quickly fell into a deep, peaceful sleep.

The next morning, I woke in the exact same position as the night before: Nestled in Adam's arms, wedged perfectly beneath his chin. Our bodies fit like gloves. I took a moment to float in suspended reality while he slept. I couldn't help but kiss his neck. He woke with a soft *Mmm. . . .*

"Good morning, beautiful," he said with a light kiss.

"Good morning," I said. Though I could swear it was all a dream.

"Did you sleep well?"

"I did. You?"

"Best sleep of my life. I knew it would be." Adam held me for a moment. "Know what the best part of waking up together is?"

"What's that?" I asked.

"Morning breath kisses!" He smothered me with his slimy, stinky lips and we wrestled around in laughter. Soon wrestling became tickling, tickling became groping, and, well. . .you get the idea.

To know me is to associate me with a coffee in my hand, and by the time I finished my shower, Adam had one ready for me. Like so many things, he knew how I liked it without the need for me to tell him, although he refused to add enough Splenda out of principle. He swore it was for my own good and could cite any number of studies that claimed sugar substitutes were toxic. He yelled that he cared about my health when I would add a packet or two more. Then I would tell him to go have another cigarette. Truth was, I simply adored the fact I mattered to him.

"What would you like to do today?" I asked as he sat down to roll a blunt.

"I'm taking you to Brooklyn. I want us to go bike riding at Prospect Park. You can bring your bike on the train and we'll stop at my place on the way to get mine."

"I'm *not* going inside your apartment." I stated flat out.

"Why?" he asked confused.

What confused me was why he had to ask. Did he seriously expect me to go in the home he built with Beth, especially while she was out of town? I felt dirty he even considered it and instantly the conversation changed tones.

"That's your home with *her*." I couldn't even say her name. "I won't disrespect this woman further by entering her home without her knowledge."

"It's just to get my bike and see my cats."

"That's not the point and you know it."

"Fine, you can stay outside while I go in, deal?"

I hesitated. It seemed a fine compromise, but something about being so close to his other life got under my skin. Adam eventually saw I was annoyed.

"Look," he approached softly, "I really want to show you the park and Brooklyn. I get your point about the house, so just wait outside and I'll be quick."

"Whatever. Let's just get it over with." Glad he won the argument,

Adam kissed me and squeezed me tight.

The apartment was a quick walk from the subway in Park Slope. I told Adam I'd wait for him at a deli on the corner. He begrudgingly agreed and showed up 15 minutes later with his bike. Together, we rode off with him in the lead.

Through a cloudless sky the sun accentuated lush greens and reflective ponds. A soft breeze filled the Saturday air and crowds of people congregated along the various paths. Several dirt trails led to hidden nooks where lovers picnicked. Open fields showed families at play and friends sprawled out on blankets catching rays.

"It's just around this bend," yelled Adam in the lead, with a specific destination in mind.

We pulled over to a grassy area and set our bikes against a tree.

"It's over here!" Adam took my hand, excited.

A few steps further and the view took my breath away. The trees, water, sun and sky all merged to create a picturesque representation of nature. Like we were at the tip of the park with infinite beauty up ahead.

"Well?" he asked.

"It's spectacular, Adam."

"I'm glad I got to bring you here. I found this spot a few months back and ever since I wanted to do this."

"Do what?" I asked.

In classic Hollywood fashion, Adam scooped me in his arms and gave me a kiss with enough *Va-va-voom* to launch a rocket. He pulled back slowly, and gazed in my eyes. "I wanted to do what feels so natural to me, in a place surrounded by nature."

Once again, he surprised me. "You're quite the *romantic*," I said with a smile. *Attractive quality number three. . . .*

We spent the afternoon together relaxing in the shade on our own version of a deserted island. We talked more about who we were, our hopes and dreams. Adam had his share of turmoil growing up. He described his mother as "crazy" and more like his sister or friend. They had smoked pot together and she had a bit of history with drug abuse during Adam's youth. He had been to his share of Narcotics and Alcoholics Anonymous meetings before he even hit his teens. When his grandmother got sick, his mother ended up in a mental hospital and he had to visit her between chemo visits with Ruth. Add to that his lack of a steady, paternal presence, no siblings to share his pain and a mind stocked with artistic genius. I could barely understand how he kept his sanity. If only I heeded those signs. Instead, I considered his survival heroic. Subconsciously, I wanted to be the mommy he didn't have. I wanted to kiss his boo-booed heart and make it all go away.

It was getting late and we were both hungry. "Come on," said Adam. "I know exactly where I want to take you for dinner. The best fish and chips you'll ever have...EVER."

"Fun! I never had fish and chips."

"I like being your first *anything*," said Adam.

He was right. To this day, it's the best fish and chips I ever ate, and he was definitely my first in that category. But now, all these years later it's not just the food I remember. It's the sheer joy of each and every moment spent that day. I loved, loved, LOVED being with Adam, whether we were talking, eating, bike riding, disagreeing, or being lazy. I loved every second.

The sun barely set and we were sweaty from the day's events. Adam's last plan for the day was for us to see a Burlesque show in Coney Island, another 45 minutes deep into Brooklyn. Too tired to protest and fairly excited for the night to continue, I let him convince me to shower at his apartment, yes the apartment I previously refused to enter.

It was a large, one bedroom apartment with ample space and high ceilings. I tiptoed inside, refusing to go anywhere but straight to the bathroom and back out the door once done. When I entered, two Siamese cats approached in their curious way to see what new female came through the door. Beth had brought them by the gym when they were kittens and though I hadn't seen them since then, Adam spoke about them all the time. Adam was the only man I ever met that loved cats as much as I did. (*Attractive quality number four.*)

After a quick hello to the kitties, Adam directed me through the kitchen to the bathroom. I noticed one of those mini magnet photo frames with a posed picture of him and Beth on the refrigerator. For the first time all day I felt angry. A small stab to my heart reminded me that no matter what I thought I felt, this man was married and that fact was unlikely to change.

As I undressed, I noticed a set of his and her robes hanging on the back hook of the bathroom door. More evidence of a grownup life already established. I started wondering what my life with Adam would be like and then reprimanded myself for such a thought. I was not allowed to let my mind go there. This was one day, among one week, for one chance with a man who lit up my world in a new way. That's all it could be. That's all it would be.

That night, safely outside the city, Adam and I hooted and hollered as we watched a bunch of voluptuous women entertain us in their pasties. Adam even volunteered for an audience contest skit where he had to perform the best "sneeze." He didn't come close to winning, but to see him venture so far out of his comfort zone, with a great sense of humor about it melted me inside. Afterward, as we rode the train home to my apartment, I fell asleep in Adam's arms like a child with her father after a day at the zoo.

The night air woke me up on the walk from the train to my front door. We held hands as we shared tidbits from the day.

"I had such a good time!" I said, fiddling with my key.

"Me, too," said Adam.

We quietly climbed the flight of stairs, and I let us inside. Without a word, Adam kissed me deeply. Something different passed between us. Over the course of our day, a new feeling that neither of us could explain had come into the mix, yet both of us undeniably felt.

We made love for the first time that night. We didn't use a condom either. We were intoxicated by emotion, oblivious to rational thought, and when we finished, there was no regret. All that remained was desire Adam eloquently expressed in one word. He held me close when it was over and whispered in my ear, "*More. . . .*"

When I think back to the week we spent together, I can recall few conversations in perfect detail. What remains unchanged is the feeling that grew inside me for this man. We filled the rest of our days with walks around the village, eating *shwarmas* from Mamoon's and standing in line for cupcakes at Magnolia Bakery. We took bike rides along the Hudson River and spent the afternoon in Central Park, sharing ice cream cones at Sheep Meadow. We went to see the Bodies exhibit at South Street Seaport, and we made love each night in a different way.

On our last day, Beth called to say she would be home early in the morning. This made another full night together impossible, and at last the reality of our parting ways hit home. I tried my best to be strong, but as Adam hugged and kissed me goodbye, I couldn't help but shed a tear. He quickly pressed his lips to my dampened cheek.

"What are you doing?" I asked.

"Swallowing your tears. Please don't cry."

"I knew this would happen!" I said, admitting I'd let things go too far.

"We need to cherish the time we spent together. I will *always* cherish this time with you," said Adam.

"And I with you." I lingered for another moment in his arms.

When he left, I closed the door and wept for our dreaded end, unaware it was only the beginning.

CHAPTER 6

❖

WHAT HAD STARTED AS A PRIMAL URGE for one kiss became a need for Adam and me to spend our lives together. Within weeks, we had expressed our love for each other, and he had decided to leave Beth. However, a year later they were still sharing a home while I remained a secret.

We tried several times to end it. I believed in my heart that we needed time apart before we could truly be together. It wouldn't be wise for Adam to go from one serious relationship to another without a chance to catch his breath. I certainly didn't want left-over Beth baggage when we finally embarked on our own chapter of life.

Most of the time he agreed with me; then a few days later he'd come back, and the cycle would repeat itself, each attempt obliterated by Adam's refusal to let me go.

You may wonder why I allowed myself to stay quiet. If I wanted my chance with Adam so badly and had already proved I would ignore my own ethical impulses to have him, why not just go tell Beth what had happened? Odds were she would choose to leave him.

I didn't want to get Adam that way. In fact, I think a mistress who tells the wife or girlfriend is a coward. We know what we're getting involved in from day one, even if we're too stupid at the time to fully understand the potential risk involved for so many. If a man left a woman to be with me, it had to be on his terms, not mine. He needed to be sure—otherwise I would never know whether it was me he wanted or that I had won his heart by a process of elimination. As long as it's an honest choice, I can handle the pain of any outcome.

Once Adam and I started sleeping together, he steadily withdrew intimacy from Beth. Every woman knows this type of behavior triggers loud warning signals, and Beth was no dummy. She quickly put two and two together and often accused Adam of having feelings for me, but he denied it. By the time Adam ceased having sex with her altogether, she needed to see a psychiatrist to make sense of it all. She urged Adam to go for counseling, but he refused. She offered to take couples sex classes, begged him to tell her what was wrong so she could fix it, but he said nothing. At night, she ran the bathroom faucet to muffle the sound of her cries. They barely spoke. They hardly touched. Whatever guilt or pain Adam felt, he buried somewhere within. In his mind, he had a plan . . .a *process*.

"Why don't you just tell her the truth?" I asked him.

"I can't!" he yelled. "I finally convinced her I *don't* have feelings for you. If she finds out I do, it will destroy her. I seriously think she might kill herself or something. You don't understand! She already feels inferior to you."

"But at least it's a *reason*!" I shouted back. "Now, she just thinks she's going insane, that you've simply stopped loving her over *nothing*. How can you *do* this to her? She needs to *know!*"

"Look, I'm doing this my way. I can't hurt her like that. She doesn't deserve it."

"Oh, but she deserves to be lied to," I shouted, "cheated on, and made a fool of when she knows in her gut she's right? Do you have any idea what it's like to feel something so deeply to be true, and the one you trust most tells you it's a lie? It's torture! No wonder she's sick over it."

"Believe me, it's better this way. I'll continue to withdraw from her. I'll keep refusing to talk or work on our relationship, and she'll get the point and move on." He met my gaze. "*She* needs to leave *me*. I can't be the one to leave her. I won't be able to live with myself."

"And what about *me?*" I demanded. "I'm supposed to just keep sneaking around in secret, worrying about Beth's feelings while mine are set aside till you see fit?"

He sighed heavily and took my hand. "Don't you see you've already won? You have my heart. You're the one I want to spend my life with. We have our whole future together. I need to make sure Beth is taken care of, and all of this goes smoothly, if you and I want to start at our best."

"What about your birthday?" I asked. "July 27 is a Friday this year. I want us to do something special."

"We have plenty of birthdays to look forward to—and *every* day with you is special."

"Actually, Adam, no one ever really knows how much time is left. We need to embrace the moment while we have it."

"It won't be long now," he said. "I promise."

The weekend of his birthday was my last closeout as general manager for the gym. Greener pastures awaited me as an operations manager for a tourist attraction in Rockefeller Center. Adam had left the gym a year before to pursue a career in real estate. He called it his first step towards world peace, since Jews and Muslims dominated the ownership market in New York City. Besides his cultural advantages, Adam's father had used his Persian rug business to teach his son the art of negotiation when he was a boy. For Adam, real estate was the perfect fit.

When Adam resigned, I had worried that it meant the end of us. We had relied on our workday for most of our time together. Instead, he'd bought a membership. We met up during workouts, between rental appointments, and after work whenever he could. Technically, Beth still had dibs on special occasions, but when the weekend of his birthday arrived, Adam stopped by the gym to surprise me. I walked him out when he left, and we shared a cigarette in one of our usual spots around the corner. I still used caution with him in public, since Beth worked nearby, though the more Adam fell for me, the less he seemed to care what others saw. A blind man could see the love for me in his eyes when we spoke. I'd often have to remind him not to be so obvious. He'd even steal a kiss now and then just to see my eyes widen in anxiety. He loved to get a rise out of me.

We huddled in a nook on the corner of University and Thirteenth Street, next to a deli. With my back against the wall, Adam stood inches away, a lovesick puppy on the verge of a kiss. His smile so big, he looked high. Stars wrapped in hearts hovered over us like a cartoon, and for just a moment, I let down my guard. At precisely that moment, I caught the familiar stare of someone over Adam's shoulder. Tingles shot through my body. I hoped for a moment that it was an illusion brought on by guilt. It wasn't.

Beth kept walking steadily towards us on University. She must have seen us the whole time. There was no chance to warn Adam. She'd seen me see her. Any sudden movement or change in behavior would be a dead giveaway we were up to no good. Time moved in slow motion as the air filled with tension.

I managed to open my mouth before she reached us. "Hi, Beth!" I shouted.

Adam thought I was joking.

"Hello there, you two!" she said with a smile. Adam gulped at the sound of her voice behind him.

"Hey," said Adam as he nervously turned around. "What are you doing here?"

To this day, I have no idea how she handled herself with such aplomb. If I had felt what she had been feeling for all those months, and seen what she had just seen, there's no way in hell I could've kept it together and put on the show she did.

"Well, honey," she answered sweetly, "remember this morning when you gave me money, so I could go to La Petit Croquet to get a gift for Sarah's bridal shower?"

"Yeah," said Adam.

"I was able to find her a present and had enough cash left over to get myself something special." She smiled seductively. "I hope you don't mind."

"N-no, that's fine."

"So, Amanda," she said, "what's new with you?"

"Not too much." My legs felt like jelly. "Sorry to run, but I gotta get back to the gym. It's the end of the month—I can't be gone too long."

"Good luck hitting your budget! It was great to see you," said Beth. Then she put the proverbial cherry on the sundae: She leaned in and gave me a hug. Adam's face read shame.

I cringed inside as I replied, "You too, Beth."

She took Adam's hand, and they walked off toward the train while I hung my head in disgrace all the way back to the gym. I recalled Adam's words on the state of their relationship and what he'd said Beth believed about us. Not for one second did she imply any of it. She had kept her composure so well, I thought that he had been lying all along and never had any intention to leave. When he failed to call that night, I played into her hands and let my mind run away with me. I imagined her home with him in some sexy lingerie number as I stared into my mirror at a fool.

The next day, Adam came by my place, and my flair for drama reared its ugly head. In my defense, I had been up all night with visions of Adam, Beth, and the lies I had decided he'd told me, convincing myself there was no way she could've stayed so cool if she really thought Adam and I were involved.

"You're a fucking *liar!*" I yelled. "You guys are *fine!*"

"No, Amanda, you're wrong."

"Whatever! . . . Why didn't you call? You were too busy fucking her in the Petit Croquet lingerie you *'gave her money for'*?"

"You have no idea how bad things were last night," said Adam. "She saw us together. She knows how I feel about you."

"You told her?"

"No, she just knows."

"Did you confirm it?" I asked.

"No, but trust me, she *knows.*"

"Bullshit! Do you have *any* idea how hard that was for me? Do you know what I put myself through all night?" My heart was racing. My hands shook. I felt desperate.

"I know. I'm sorry."

"You're *not* sorry! You just let this go on and on. It's all about how Beth feels. What about how *I* feel? Do you even care about how I feel?"

He remained quiet. His lack of reaction infuriated me. How could I possibly get his attention? How could I make him see how much he was hurting me? I grabbed a butcher knife from the kitchen drawer and held it close to me.

"You're so worried about her killing herself? What about me? Would you care if I did that?" I wailed.

"Amanda, *stop!*" he barked, loudly and deeply enough to snap me out of my hysteria. He grabbed my wrist, and the knife fell. His eyes were scared. I knew I had taken it way too far.

"I wasn't gonna do it," I said, calming down.

"Well, you can't even fucking play like that! You can never do that again! I won't be with someone who does that!"

"Don't you see?" I asked. "You're making all of us crazy!"

"I know," he said, frustrated. "But after yesterday, this will all be over soon."

It turned out he had spoken the truth. Within days, Beth had told him she was done trying, that she knew there was no hope left for them. She volunteered to move out, and divorce proceedings began. Finally, the light at the end of our tunnel of love started to appear. Soon all the pain would be worth it.

CHAPTER 7

❖

Adam was a huge fan of anything ancient, historical, or out of this world. In September 2007, he received an ample commission from a real estate deal. As a reward, he decided to fulfill one of his lifelong dreams to visit Egypt.

Beth had finally found an apartment and was planning to move out while he was gone. It seemed things had finally started to turn our way. I'd begun a new job with great people and soon I'd be able to shout my love for Adam from a rooftop.

He and I agreed, though, to preserve the facade of our platonic friendship for the time being. News would break of the divorce, and after some time people would believe two close friends found love. The truth ran the risk of hurting Beth and labeling me a home-wrecker.

I admit I was nervous with Adam halfway across the world. I hadn't spent more than a few days apart from him in over three years. On top of that, I'd only lately had the freedom to love him. I worried his plane would go down, or he'd connect with his roots and fall in love with the desert. He used to say he had a fantasy in which he walked along the sand and fell into a cave where a white Bengal tiger would approach him and lead him on some mystical journey. Adam's father descended from a prominent bloodline in Iran, and Adam yearned to travel there, but his father refused to let him. Back then, Adam knew why. Now, all these years later, so do I. At the time, all I knew was what Adam told me, which wasn't much. His family name carried enough weight to put him in a position where he might effect the kind of social change he dreamed about, should he choose to pursue a permanent life there. I assumed his dad didn't want to send his only son all the way across the world. I certainly didn't want Adam choosing world peace over *us*. A couple of times he'd asked me if I would be his "*Iranian Princess.*" God help me, I'd said yes. I would've lived in Siberia with Adam if he'd asked me to by then. I'd waited so long for my prince I would be his princess *anywhere*. We were too close to turn back.

I can't recall whether it was a week or ten days that Adam was gone. I only remember the agony of being apart from him. He sent me a brief email during a stopover in Amsterdam, on the day of his return, with two pictures attached: one webcam shot of him smoking a joint in a coffee shop, and the other with him dressed in full Egyptian garb, riding a camel under the hot sun. He looked one hundred percent native in the sand and absolutely beautiful. I wanted to change my name to Jasmine and go on his magic carpet ride. The only thing missing was the tiger seated at his feet. I stared at the picture on my computer, daydreaming of when I could see him again, when I noticed his left hand—more specifically his left *ring finger*—was bare. I zoomed in to get a better look, and sure enough, Adam had removed his wedding ring. This was it! A sure sign his marriage was over and we were finally able to begin. I literally cried tears of joy. I couldn't wait to see him. I imagined we would celebrate by first ripping each other's clothes off, and catch up on stories later.

To my disappointment, I received quite a different reaction when he finally appeared at my door. I had imagined he would lift me up and spin me around in a passionate kiss, like a sailor returned home from the war. In reality, he gave me a measly "Hi," a quick kiss, and barely a hug. Something was. . . *off*. Our clothes stayed on the entire time, and I was forced to see a thousand pictures of a vacation I hadn't taken. I noticed a certain girl in a few of them and wondered if she the cause of his coldness.

"Who's that?" I asked him, pointing to the girl.

"We took the camels to the pyramids, and she was part of the group that went. She was cool," he said.

"Did something happen between you two?"

"No!" he answered, his voice shocked and annoyed. "You're not gonna do this every time you see me with a girl, are you? I really don't like jealousy in my relationship."

First of all, I'm female and Puerto Rican. My DNA is predisposed to a certain level of jealousy. Second, an occupational hazard of being the other woman is the constant awareness your man is capable of cheating: If he did it to her with you, he can do it to you with someone else. However, neither of those forces inspired my insecurity. It was his *behavior*. There we were, an illicit couple finally free to embrace their love, parted for days and now back in each other's arms, and he had barely made an effort to touch me.

"I have a lot on my mind," he said. "I came home, and Beth is gone. I'm glad she's gone, but the reality is I'm going through a divorce. Legal ties, family ties. . . . It's not all so simple."

"Look." I approached him tenderly. "You know I always said it would be tough to jump from one relationship to the next. Maybe we should take a break for a bit, until you get everything in order."

Adam softened. "No. That's not what I want. I want *you*." He sat me on his lap. "I just need you to understand if I don't always act how you want me to with all this. Don't assume the worst."

I felt silly. "Okay, I understand." My already thin patience had to hang on a bit longer.

A few weeks later, a leasing manager position opened up with my parent company in a prominent residential development on the east side of Manhattan. My company was owned by one of the world's leading global real estate developers, and it was a perfect opportunity for Adam. He had flourished financially where he was and quickly earned recognition as a top agent. But the thought of steady income, benefits, and limitless growth potential made him apply for the leasing manager job. (And I would get a hefty bonus if he was hired.)

It never occurred to me he might get passed over. It never occurred to him either. He always achieved, succeeded, got what he wanted. It was simply a matter of time.

He aced the first three interviews and felt sure the fourth was just a formality. He wound down his rental business in prep for the transition. He didn't want to start working with clients and then have to drop them. He had a tremendous work ethic. As his boss I had seen it first-hand. He was prompt, reliable, gave great service, and contributed to the team.

My father had owned a real estate company for most of his life. Real estate is a 24/7 business, and my time with Adam was often shared with his Blackberry. Landing the position with my firm meant another step towards a normal life with the man I loved.

"How'd it go?" I asked him when he returned from his final interview.

He looked disturbed. "Umm. . .*okay*. They said they'd let me know."

"Just okay?" I asked.

"It was weird. The guy who interviewed me, Mr. Tejada, was *weird*."

I knew Tejada by reputation. He'd started in my branch of the company and worked closely with several of my co-workers. "Difficult" and "challenging" are kind words to describe his professional demeanor. "I warned you he was a hard-ass. It was probably just his personality. Come to mama." I sat Adam on my bed and moved in behind him to rub his shoulders.

He sat down willingly. "Maybe. . . ."

". . .What is it?" I prodded.

"Well. . .he asked me why I wanted to be a leasing manager. So I told him all about my art and my achievements. My hopes of growth, and how this would give me the opportunity to achieve my long-term goals."

"Yeah, and. . . ?"

"And he said, '*What's that have to do with leasing?*'

"Ouch," I said.

"Exactly. He had that type of attitude the whole time."

"Babe, it's probably not as bad as you think. I thought I flopped on my final interview with Beverly, and I still got the job. The others really liked you. I'm sure it'll be fine." I kissed his neck.

"I love you, Amanda."

"I love you, too."

"No," he said seriously. He turned around to face me. "I *really* love you. I've never felt this way in my life."

After we made love, we took a shower. We held each other close and enjoyed the sound of the water as it fell upon us.

"You're never gonna leave me, right?" he asked out of nowhere.

"Of course not!" I gazed up at him. "What made you ask that?"

"I don't know." I sensed he meant to say more but couldn't find the words. I also saw tears form in his eyes. ". . . What's wrong, Adam?"

"I don't ever want to lose you," he answered.

"Aww." I melted. "You won't lose me. After the fight I put up to get you? Hell no, I don't think so."

"You say that now, but. . .you never know. I mean. . . something may happen."

"Like what?" I asked.

"Anything!" he answered defensively. Part of me thought

he *wanted* me to admit I would leave. "There may come a time where I push you away. I may say things to you I don't mean, hurtful things."

". . .And why might you do this?" I asked, confused.

"I just might! Stress. . .you never know!"

"Okay," I replied, treading lightly.

"If I do," he went on, "please don't leave. Whatever happens, know that I will never, *ever* resort to violence with you. No matter what I say, I am not a violent person, and I will never physically harm you."

"Okay, honey," I said softly.

He hugged me tight. "*Thank you*," he whispered.

"Don't worry about the job. You're truly a great man, capable of wonderful things. I believe in you."

He cried as he held me. "Sometimes it's so hard, knowing what I have to do and the road to get there."

It felt as if we had suddenly changed topics and he'd forgotten to fill me in. He was telling me he didn't want to lose me, yet I simultaneously thought *he* might end things. "Is this 'something' you have to do. . .is it something you have to do *alone*?" I asked.

"Some have told me I'm better off alone. But I don't want to be alone, Amanda. So please. . .*never leave*."

If you're wondering whether any alarms went off in my head at this interaction, *absolutely*. Yes, he seemed unusually sad after the interview. Yes, his talk of potentially turning on me to some extent, for no reason, made little sense. Yes, random tears surprised me. Never underestimate the power of the human mind to rationalize its way to a desired response.

Vague recollections of stories he told me about events in his past flitted across my mind. The time he tried Ecstasy and didn't come down for two weeks. Another time around high school or college, something similar had happened when he tried cocaine. He was medicated at the time but had been off meds for seven years, though I never asked what those meds were for. Mostly I remembered funny anecdotes he told his friends as entertainment, the way one recalls drunken exploits from a party. A few years ago, I fell in love with the show Mad Men. In Season Four, in the episode "Summer Man," Don Draper says: *"People tell you who they are, but we ignore it—because we want them to be who we want them to be."* Loving Adam blinded me.

CHAPTER 8

❖

T HE SUBTLE CHANGES in Adam's behavior continued through the holidays and into the start of 2008. Several weeks had passed since his final interview with my company, and he'd received no answer either way. He'd reached out to the contacts from the earlier interviews, but they hadn't returned his calls. It wasn't the type of company to drop the ball or leave someone in limbo. I spoke with my Human Resources contact for the organization and explained the situation. She apologized profusely and, by the end of the day, confirmed that Adam had not gotten the position: Strike One.

"Can you believe they tried to say they left me a *message?*" Adam shouted. "My phone is on my hip every minute of the day. They did *not* leave me a message!"

"Calm down, Adam."

"They can't *do* this! They can't string someone along, cause them to lose business, and *lie!*"

I hadn't seen that side of him before. Tantrums were *my* thing, not his. "Adam!" I shouted back. "*Calm down!*"

He sat on the bed and put his head in his hands. When I approached, he threw his arms around my waist and cried into my belly as

I stood before him.

"Shh," I whispered. "It's gonna be okay. It's not like you don't have a job at all."

"No," he said, "you don't understand. I already told them I was leaving. I gave away most of my leads."

". . .Why would you do that if you weren't certain?" I asked, confused. He knew better than to leave without a solid offer.

He pulled away from me sharply and shot me an enemy look. "*Really?* You're really gonna say you told me so *now?*"

"I wasn't saying that, Adam. It's unlike you to take that type of step before knowing for sure."

"Well, I thought I knew." He stood up suddenly. "I don't need this from you, Amanda. You're supposed to make me feel better, and you're just telling me what an idiot I am." He put on his shoes and collected his things.

"You're *leaving?*" I asked stupefied.

"Yes, I'm leaving." He grabbed his coat, kissed my cheek, and walked out before I could react.

What the hell just happened? I asked myself. *One minute he's planning to spend the night, the next he's bawling like a baby, and now he's gone?* I suddenly remembered a straight-A student in my seventh-grade math class who once failed a quiz. He ripped up the quiz and ate it while he cried at his desk. Overachievers climb high, but they have a long way to fall, and their pain runs disturbingly deep.

Adam didn't speak to me until the next evening. He showed up at my apartment as if nothing had happened.

"Let's make up," he said, pulling me close for a kiss.

"No," I said as I tried to pull away.

"C'mon, gorgeous. I missed you."

"You think you can walk out, ignore me, and then show up here like all is well?"

"I'm sorry," said Adam, "but I was really down, and you were being unsupportive."

He had to be kidding. I replayed the events in my mind, going back to the day I first told him of the position. I'd done nothing *but* support him!

"You really believe that?" I asked in shock.

"Oh, come on, admit it." He said it with a smile on his face, as if I were a little kid who wouldn't confess she'd broken a lamp.

". . .Adam, I've supported you every step of the way."

"Yes, you have." He kissed my neck.

"Stop it! I'm serious."

"I know!" He mocked my tone. "You're very serious. I'm serious, too." He kissed the other side of my neck, and moved his hand to the small of my back, pressing my lady parts against him. I felt warm below the waist. *Oh, dear. . . .*

Ten seconds later I was in his arms, off the ground and rushed to my bed. We barely took our lips off each other to breathe between kisses. It felt like being caught in a brushfire as the fire itself. Adam consumed me with a different force behind him. He pulled at my shirt and bra to expose my breasts. His teeth grazed my nipple and caused my back to arch in pleasurable pain. He yanked my leggings and underwear to my knees. Before I knew it he was inside me, pressing deep, fast and hard. We screamed out in ecstasy, and our argument was over. Adam and I lay on the bed, huffing and puffing without words, my pants entwined at my ankles, my shirt and bra in disarray, his cum on my stomach.

"Whoo!" he cried out, rejuvenated with energy I couldn't comprehend. He jumped from the bed and handed me some tissues to clean up, then reached for his Blackberry and sat naked in the chair as he checked his email.

Not only did I probably look like a prostitute, I suddenly felt like one. Adam always snuggled after sex; it was like mentally making love after the physical part was over. Rather than relaxed, he was more amped up than when we started, and I felt a distance growing between us.

"Are you okay?" I hoped for a response to put me at ease.

"Yup! Just need to check something. . . ." He didn't bother to look up.

I rolled my eyes the way women do about men and convinced myself we were settling in as a couple. Maybe post-sex snuggles were no longer required. They had been necessary when our time together was limited; we had relied on them to get us through our time apart. Now there was no pressure to savor each moment as our last. In many ways we were beginning, but in reality we had slept together for almost two years. I convinced myself that his lackluster attitude meant we had reached a new level of "comfort" as people do when relationships evolve.

I caught a glimpse of myself in the mirror as I turned towards the bathroom. When I think back to describe it, my reflection takes a life of its own and tells me, *This is not you.* But if it actually told me so that night, I promise you I ignored it. Somewhere under my skin, in my mind, or embedded in the cosmic planes around us, I *knew* something wasn't right. Adam had been rough; I told myself it was hot, make-up sex. He had been distant; I told myself it meant we were getting closer. My big-picture fantasy of a perfect, normal relationship with him was all I let myself see, oblivious to any truth that might reveal exactly what it was: *a fantasy.* From day one, he, and our relationship, were anything but normal. It's what in part sucked me in. Yet despite the endless warning signs of what lay ahead, I chose the fantasy of *normal.*

As I finished up in the bathroom, I heard Adam's phone ring through the door. Thanks to Beth, the sound sent Pavlovian chills down my spine. Since she rarely called anymore, and never that late, it could only be one other person: *Adam's mother, Peggy.* Within seconds, the elevated volume of his voice confirmed it.

When I was in first grade, I read a story about a little girl who had a dream she was given the chance to choose her parents before being born. When she woke up, she realized the parents she had chosen, of all the people in the world, were the ones she already had. That pretty much sums up how I feel about my family. Daddy issues aside, despite a few tearful Thanksgivings and arguments on Christmas, I wouldn't trade my family for anything. Our laughter and love rise above all life's challenges, and my quest for the dysfunctional normal stems from an unconditional love I have felt since birth. My family is my life. My mother is the strongest, most loving, forgiving, innocent, yet wise woman I know. Her children are her world. Our happiness is all that matters, and she spends each of her days praying for us, supporting us, and loving us no matter who or what comes our way. Soon you'll see more of what I mean.

Adam's mother, Peggy, was another story.

Like it or not, parents are directly responsible for part of the adult their child becomes, from a blessing to a burden. My father had difficulty expressing emotion with those closest to him, and yes, it was a factor in most of my adult decisions, especially after he died of lung cancer when I was twenty-two.

As I approach forty, I know my life is ultimately my creation and my decisions are mine alone. Now, I understand that my father had his own issues and left too early for us to find our way through them. For many years, I let my father's ghost guide me down a bunch of wrong paths by throwing blame for my life in his direction. The truth of the matter is, though, I never once doubted my father's love for me, and he worked hard to provide for us. God bless him, no man ever made me feel safer. And at the end of the day when I reflect, that's really all that matters.

The more I learned of Adam's twisted maternal dynamic, the more I understood the basis for his individual challenges, and the more I wanted to fill the void his mother left behind. I found overcoming adversity extremely sexy. The fact that Adam had turned out so ambitious and loving, with a mother suffering from a mental disorder and drug addiction, boggled my mind and turned me on. He accepted his role as the adult in their relationship and willingly let me nurture him. In fact, I think that was part of his plan from the start.

During our first two years as friends, I had met Peggy once when she came from Florida to visit him and Beth. Beth kept her entertained while Adam was working, and they stopped by the gym to say hello.

A few months after we began our affair, I met Peggy again when I took a long weekend trip to Miami with a friend of mine. Since there was no chance of Adam going with me, he wanted to be part of it any way he could, so he asked his mom to get me a family rate at a prominent hotel where she worked. No one but Beth thought anything of it.

In my head, when I went to thank Peggy in person for our discounted room, I was thanking my future mother-in-law and made sure to be on my best behavior. A mother knows when a woman loves her son, and I took effort to control my emotion when I saw traces of Adam in her face.

Peggy had been a big fan of Beth, but over a year later, when Adam explained the divorce and his love for me, she welcomed me with open arms—arms so open, in fact, I detected her peculiarity. She said anything that came across her mind, without a filter. She would tell me she was happy for Adam and me, but that she felt bad for Beth. She went on and on about any topic under the sun, and when I relayed her tales to Adam, he'd tell me, "She lies," and to ignore her. He loved her and hated her at the same time. She called at all hours to ramble on about nothing, and if he didn't answer, she kept calling. All conversations started out fine, but if they lasted more than two minutes, drama ensued. One day, I finally asked Adam what the deal was between him and his mother. They say a woman can predict the kind of husband a man will be from how he treats his mother, and so far, things didn't bode well. That was when he told me she suffered from bipolar disorder.

Suddenly, his trips with her, as a boy, to Narcotics and Alcoholics Anonymous meetings made sense. His description of feeling more like a parent than a child clicked in a new way. The laughs on the surface about smoking pot with his mom revealed scars buried like a dark curse. A small bell, the ding of a triangle in a wall of orchestral sound, went off in my head.

"Doesn't that run in families?" I asked.

"There was a time they thought *I* might have it, back when that shit happened with the drugs I told you about," he said. "I was on meds for a little while, but I haven't taken anything in seven years and I'm fine, so the doctors said it's probably not the same thing."

If questions start popping up in your head as you read this, I confess that I'm sharing this story so that, if you ever find yourself in this situation, you not only ask for, but *demand,* greater detail.

I didn't.

When the phone rang that night as I was cleaning up in the bathroom and convincing myself that all was well, Peggy was calling to pressure Adam on a financial matter involving the Miami home his grandmother had left to them both when she died. Peggy shared the home with her Cuban drunk of a husband, Ricardo. Adam had never liked him, and though Ricardo often contributed to Peggy's chaos, he also shared it. At least with Ricardo at her side, Peggy wasn't alone. Besides, Adam understood his mother's ability to drive one to drink.

"Why are you calling me now?" Adam asked loudly. ". . .But why *now?* . . . I don't care what Ricardo wants, it's not his fucking house!"

"Adam! *Please*," I whispered. "It's almost midnight. I have neighbors." If he heard me, he didn't care. He continued to shout, "What are you *talking* about? You're making no sense! Why won't you be able to work? What doctor?"

Suddenly, he grew quiet. His eyes turned red and glassy. ". . .And when is your appointment?"

Something was wrong. I saw an angry man wither to a frightened boy with barely a muscle moving. I left the room to offer privacy and returned only when I heard him say good-bye.

". . .Is everything alright?" I asked.

"My mother." He paused. "She has breast cancer."

"Oh, my God!" I ran to him.

I sat in his lap and held him close to my heart while he cried. (Strike Two.)

Over the next few weeks, Adam worked non-stop to rebuild the rental business he had lost when he applied for the other job. Free time became non-existent, along with the quality time we spent together when he wasn't on the worldwide web. If I complained, he told me he was building a life for us, and I accepted any answer geared in that direction. Adam appeared to be handling his mother's cancer well, though he didn't mention it unless I asked. When I did, he kept his answers brief. I figured work helped take his mind off things, and that he knew I was there if he wanted me. Still, I felt a need for attention I was no longer getting, and during an attempt to crawl between Adam and his laptop for some tender lovin' care, he flicked me away with his hand, and it set me off. "What the fuck is your problem?" I asked.

"Nothing!" he snapped back. "I'm just. . .working."

I huffed off the bed. "Something has been up with you since Egypt!" I barked.

"You don't know what you're talking about."

"It's true. Since you came home, you've been different with me. *Something* happened there that I know you're not telling me." I refused to budge till I had an answer.

He put the computer aside and sat up. "You're right," he said. "I have been keeping something from you."

My heart sank.

"When I was in Egypt. . . . I did cocaine."

"What? With whom?"

"With some people there."

"With that *girl?*"

". . .And some others."

"Did something *happen* with her?"

"Absolutely not," he assured me.

". . .Why didn't you tell me?" I finally asked, betrayed.

"Because I know how you feel about it, and I knew you'd be angry."
He sounded so honest it stunted my reaction.

"Have you done it since?"

"A few times," he admitted. "That's why sometimes I've been kind
of anxious around you. It makes me that way, and I was nervous you'd
catch on."

"Whom did you do it with here?" I already had an idea of what he'd
say.

"Naz, Tyler, and Nick." His boys.

"Aren't you *not supposed* to do that shit? Isn't that the cause of those
issues you had in your past?"

"Yeah, but that was different."

"How?"

He brushed it off. "There were other circumstances involved back
then. Anyway, that's why I've been weird with you at times. I felt guilty
that you didn't know about it."

He was one smart motherfucker. One time, during a conversation
about the importance of honesty, I told him what my mother had told
me about truth when I was eight years old: "You can tell me any truth:
I may scream or get mad, but I'll always respect you and I'll always forgive you. But lie to me once, and I'll never believe you again." My poor
mother had heard many difficult answers to questions asked over the
years because of that statement. She kept her word and always forgave

me no matter how angry or disappointed she felt.

Adam was also right about my feelings towards cocaine. He knew I took pride in the fact I had never tried it. I'd always thought that, if I did, one of two things would happen: Either I would try it once and die like Len Bias (which I couldn't risk for my mother's sake), or I would end up an addict pimped out on the street for some blow. Plus, I always felt if my life ever sank to the level where I needed to snort something up my nose for recreation, it meant an immediate change was necessary. Several of my friends, in various chapters of my life from college to my time at the gym, had dabbled with coke. I'm not declaring myself innocent by any means. I've tried Ecstasy and mushrooms a handful of times over the years. I once spent twelve days in Amsterdam that took me nine months to mentally recover from. I had some great times and some nightmares as a result.

The idea had been to outgrow these rebel ways, and I was not about to settle down with a man who hadn't put that lifestyle behind him. My ex, Sean, had been a former addict and it was hard enough dating *him* while he was in recovery. Had I known of Adam's interest in the drug, even if he only did it occasionally on nights out with the boys, I would *never* have gotten involved. Now he had me. So he had withheld pertinent information, but now he was telling me about it with grace and dignity, in exact accordance with my truth oath. I had told him it was okay to tell me anything. I *couldn't* go back on my word. I *had* to forgive him. Told ya. . .*one smart motherfucker.*

"Adam," I said calmly, "I don't want to be with a man who does drugs like that."

"I know," he said, shamed.

"I also don't want to be with a man who keeps things from me."

"I know. I'm sorry."

"Are you prepared to grow up and let this childish, immature bullshit go?"

"For you? Definitely. I don't even want to do it anymore. It's stupid."

"Fine." I didn't yell or throw a tantrum. I put my arms around him, kissed him, and thanked him for telling me the truth.

"Why don't we stay at my place tonight?" he asked. "I'll get food from the market and cook us dinner. I want to sleep next to you in *my* bed for a change."

I hated staying in the home Adam built with Beth, but it seemed a fair shot at starting the night fresh and rewarding Honest Adam for coming clean. I quickly put together an overnight bag, gave Oliver and Lulu kisses goodnight, and we made our way to the subway.

Adam started cooking right away. It wasn't until after we ate that he noticed his cat, Hooker, breathing strangely. Adam constantly worried about her. He'd gotten Hooker and Cleopatra as babies, and Hooker was the runt of the litter. She got her name for being an attention whore. She was queen of the house, and wherever she was, Cleo was sure to be close by. Hooker loved to perch on top of the television above all else. Whenever Adam walked by, she bathed him with kisses as if she was a lioness and he her cub. Adam loved her with all his heart, and the two cats had carried him through the past few months of trying times. Aside from the labored breathing, Hooker seemed in good spirits. No big deal—Adam would take her to the vet the next morning.

I was at work when he called, sobbing, at the other end of the line.

"What is it?" I asked frantically.

"Hooker. She has heart disease. She doesn't have much longer to live."

"I'll be right over."

When I got to Brooklyn after explaining to my boss that I had an emergency, Adam's eyes were swollen, his cheeks tear-stained. He played with Hooker on his bed while he cried.

"The doctor said he doesn't know how long she has. Could be a few weeks. Could be a few months. I always knew this might happen because she was born so small. She almost didn't survive, ya know."

"I know, honey." I sat with them on the bed.

"But she was so *strong*," he whispered. Then he added with sudden vigor, "She *beat the odds!* I'm gonna pray for her."

"Good idea," I said.

Adam closed his eyes and, in a tone generated from his diaphragm, recited a prayer in Hebrew. I sincerely wish a camera had caught my reaction; not only was Adam not particularly religious, I didn't even know he could speak Hebrew. Sure, I knew he'd had a bar mitzvah once, but I imagined that was the only time he'd ever spoken the language. My face shifted from a smile to open-mouthed shock. There was nothing typical about the situation to compare it to. I know I start to cry if I even remotely *think* of something happening to my Oliver. I took his prayer as a desperate attempt to save his cat.

When he finished, I held him in my arms and stroked his head as he held Hooker close to his chest. Tiny sobs sporadically escaped him. "Everything will work out," I told him, worried I could be wrong. Hooker's illness was Strike Three, and as we all know, Strike three, and you're out. In Adam's case, it meant *out of his mind.*

CHAPTER 9

❖

B Y SPRING 2008, Adam was living at a brisk pace. He joined the
fraternity of Freemasonry and took it very seriously. Freemasons
employ historical ritual and philosophy to teach ideas such as
brotherly love, wisdom, and truth (*or so Wikipedia* claims). The most I
knew about it came from movies like *National Treasure* and *The Da Vinci
Code*, which weren't completely off the mark. The brotherhood contains
elements of mystery and secrecy geared towards the quest for knowledge.
Freemasonry incorporates art and symbolism into its studies. Many of
the members are leaders in their field, people who have had great
achievements and success, including more than a dozen U.S. presidents.
Adam claimed he had joined mostly as a networking tool, but it seemed
to serve as a portal, offering a surge of stimulation to parts of his brain
previously at rest.

At the same time, he began reading a series of books called *The Earth
Chronicles* by Zecharia Sitchin. Each several-hundred-page book provides
factual evidence for the existence of aliens and their key role in ancient
human history.

At his request, I read the first book in the series, *The Twelfth Planet*.
The extent of primeval references and astronomical data often left my

mind spinning. It took me two weeks of reading in spurts to barely digest the volume. By the time I finished, Adam was starting the seventh in the series. We had great debates over the theories. He spoke with such authority on the subject matter, I often felt like his pupil. Actually, I was more like a sponge. I absorbed him in any way or form I could. If he had told me the world was flat or the sun really the moon, I would've found a way to believe him.

I still saw Adam every day, and we spent most nights together, but our relationship filled up spaces between all the other things on his plate. Even worse, he added more whenever he could.

In early May, I had nearly reached the end of my rope when I finally heard the words I'd waited so long for.

"It's done," said Adam as he came through my door. He took his coat off and sat in the chair by the window.

"What is?" I asked, prepared for the worst.

"My marriage." He smiled. "Beth signed the papers."

"*What?*" I gasped. "You *saw* her?" I climbed on his lap.

"I found them signed when I got home. She must have dropped them off."

"Wow."

"You know what this means?" asked Adam. "We can finally be together."

"Finally!" I threw my hands in the air victoriously.

"That's right, baby." Adam scooped me in his arms. "Our future starts *now*." He made love to me that night without distraction.

The newfound freedom with Adam took some getting used to. I couldn't help but look over my shoulder each time he reached for my hand. Coming out to the public took on a life of its own, depending on who heard the news. The story we told was that we'd grown closer as his marriage broke apart, and that we had ended up falling in love.

My family, as well as Dory, a close friend of mine from the gym, had known the details from the start. They offered congratulations and wished us luck. For most people, it came as a surprise. Perhaps they felt it was too soon for Adam to move on or still imagined Adam and Beth as the happy couple they had pretended to be. How many people actually bought our story, I'll never know. A few weeks later, it wouldn't matter.

Around mid-June, Adam asked me to join him for the last session held by his Masonic lodge before they broke for the summer. It was one of the only sessions women could attend, and I couldn't help but want to get a glimpse behind that curtain. But, since Adam had begun his process so late in their season, he had to wait until fall for his official induction ceremony. After four hours without air conditioning, we went for the traditional dinner the lodge sponsored. Adam spent most of the night talking with his fellow *brothers,* while I did my best to fake a good time.

At close to midnight, we made our way to the subway and my apartment. Adam had drunk a couple of glasses of wine and was feeling mellow, going on and on about the significance of the ceremony we had seen.

His phone rang. Once again, his blood pressure quickly elevated.

When his business took a turn for the worse, he had proposed to his mother that they refinance the home they co-owned in Florida. He'd found a great rate through a major bank that would provide them with a cushion of cash in case Peggy needed to miss work due to her illness. It also gave Adam the chance to rebuild his business without panic over paying his bills. I vividly remember the phone call when Peggy agreed to it, since it had been the only time I ever saw Adam smile after speaking to her.

Now, out of nowhere, she was taking it all back. "Mom, *no!*" he shouted. "You don't know what you're doing!"

"Adam," I said, "lower your voice."

He didn't listen. He continued to scream at the top of his lungs in the middle of Twenty-third Street and Eighth Avenue. People whispered and stared as they walked by. Others shook their heads and giggled at the Only in New York scene. I completely understood his frustration, but indulging in such a public display completely violated his personal code of conduct.

"You tell fucking Ricardo he has *no say* in what we do! He's a *drunk!* He's a *scumbag!* You're an idiot for *listening* to him!"

After a few more attempts to calm him down, I finally walked off to distance myself.

He soon appeared in front of me. "C'mon, let's go." He took my hand and we turned towards the train.

"What happened?" I asked.

"She changed her mind. She's not signing for the loan. Her fucking asshole husband wants some of it, and if we don't give it to him, she won't do it at all."

"Adam, I understand that it's upsetting, but you really can't let them get to you like that."

"Don't tell me how to handle my family. It's *my* family. You stay out of it."

"I wasn't trying to get involved, I just—"

"Then don't speak about what you don't know about."

I didn't know what to say. The man had just subjected me to twenty minutes of shouting in the middle of a city street and then told me to mind my business. I was still under the impression he had become my family. "You don't want me involved? Fine," I said. "I'm gone."

I left the subway platform. I heard him call out my name, but he didn't follow.

Two avenues east, I boarded a different train back to my apartment, going over the events of the evening and Adam's attitude over the past few weeks. Somehow things had spun out of hand, but I didn't know where his anger was coming from. If I tried to talk to him about it, he blamed the chaos of his life. He told me to be patient and not make it about me. Since his feelings for me didn't seem to be in question, I accepted it as a rough time for him and did my best to be supportive.

When I got home, he was waiting outside my building. He didn't apologize; in fact, he didn't say much. I planned to give him a piece of my mind, to really let him have it. Instead, I didn't say much either. It was late and I chose to avoid further drama.

For the next couple of days, I distanced myself from him. When we were together, I focused on anything that could distract me from asking the questions I was too afraid to ask—questions about his behavior or our future that I had every right to ask yet never did, in fear of somehow disrupting the dream of our being together.

Suddenly one afternoon, I received a frantic phone call. "I want you to move in with me," said Adam.

"Aww, honey. I want that someday, too."

"I mean *now*, Amanda. I want you to move in with me *now*. Right away!"

I thought he was kidding. He knew I was two months into a new lease on my apartment. "Adam, I can't move in with you now."

"*What?* Why!"

"I can't just break my lease, Adam. Besides, what's the rush?"

"Are you *kidding* me?" He sounded angry. "After everything we've been through, and now you don't want to move in with me? This is fucking ridiculous."

His reaction completely threw me. "It's not that I don't want to live with you, it's just so soon after the papers were signed, and it's a big step. I think we should take our time—"

"You know what? Forget it. Obviously you were never really serious about this relationship."

". . .I beg your pardon?" I asked.

"I gave up my *marriage* for you! Now you're telling me you don't want to *rush* things? If this is how you feel, then let's just not bother anymore. If you don't want to move in with me, let's just end it now."

"*End it?* Are you *joking?*" I was flabbergasted; he had never behaved like this.

"I guess you're still not sure about me. I guess you don't want to give up your single lifestyle."

"Adam, I gave up my single lifestyle *two years ago!*" I yelled. "Why are you acting like this?"

"Because I sacrificed everything to be with you, and now you don't want to."

"We *talked* about this! I don't want to live in the apartment you had with Beth. We were supposed to find a place of our own together."

"Well, start out with me in Brooklyn, and we can save for a few months to get something in the city." His voice finally began to soften. "There's no need for us both to keep paying so much money when we ultimately plan to end up together. Let's just do it."

As I tell it now, it's clear as day to me that he was desperate for money. He needed someone to share his rent with, and the rest of his world clouded his ability to fully think through any type of consequence, good or bad. My world was clouded with him, and all I needed was one acceptable reason to throw caution to the wind and follow my heart.

"Okay," I said. "Let's do it!"

"Really, Amanda?"

"Yes. I don't want to waste any more time with you."

"I love you so much." He said it like he meant it.

My heart melted. "I love you too, Adam."

"Now, go call your landlord. Don't worry about the lease. You just need to give him thirty days' notice, and it should be fine."

In a euphoric state, I hung up the phone, my dream finally in the making. Adam's *process* was finally over, and the reward was mine. There was much to do in a short amount of time, but I welcomed every second of it with open arms.

My landlord wasn't happy with the news at all but agreed that, if he could find a new tenant, he would let me break the lease. With a great apartment in a prime location, I wasn't worried. However, I still needed to pack up four years of my life in a matter of days, and paint the walls I had changed to a dark color, in order to get my security deposit back. I told my landlord everything would be finished by July 1. All my free time went to weeding out papers and sifting through piles of things to keep or throw away. I don't think I ever stopped smiling as I planned for the long-awaited chapter to begin. I'd found the man I hoped for my whole life. He was my best friend. He wanted me above all else, and as the baby of my family, I embraced my chance to grow up.

A few days before the move, Adam decided it was time for him to draw again. Aside from sketches, he had not created a piece of art in eight years. When I asked him why, he never gave much of an answer. I had seen that type of behavior in other elite artists over the years. I knew dancers who devoted the first twenty-five years of their lives to ballet and then never touched a toe shoe again. I knew singers who performed half their lives and then wouldn't consider a turn at karaoke. A book I once read called *The Artist's Way* described the artistic mind as a well that dries up and begs for replenishment. I imagined that's what happened with Adam. The relevant point was that, after eight years, his well was full, and he couldn't wait to drink the water.

"I'd like you to pose for me," said Adam.

"Me?" I blushed.

"Yes. I'd like it to be nude."

"You want me to pose *nude*? I can't do that." It wasn't so much shyness holding me back as my body dysmorphia issues and a lifelong battle with my weight.

"Amanda, you're my muse. My first drawing has to be you. It has to be a figure drawing of your beautiful, naked body."

He had me at *muse*. I craved to see him as an artist in action, and I purred inside at how sexy he made me feel.

The only problem was the timing. Portraits took hours we didn't have. I had to finish packing up my apartment and paint the walls.

"Adam, I'm honored to be your subject, but now's not the time for this."

"Sure it is."

"No, honey. I have tons of things to do to get ready for the move."

"I'll help you with your apartment, you sit for my drawing. That's only fair." There was always a fine line to fairness from Adam's perspective.

"I'm not sure, with everything going on, this is a good idea."

"Amanda, I need to draw," he answered. "I've been in a period of sleep for eight years. Thanks to you and the Masons, I'm awake again. Please."

His Jedi mind-trick worked, and several hours on three of my last five nights, meant for moving, were spent naked in a leather chair, posing for Adam. The drawing came out incredible, and watching him work is a memory I treasure. He used charcoal pencils on a sheet of paper taped to the wall. He wore his glasses and took off his shirt at my request. I watched his defined muscles shape images of me out of thin air. His hypnotizing brown eyes studied every inch of me. Half-empty boxes and half-painted walls mattered little to me. I marveled at his willingness to immortalize, me and I reveled in being the source of his inspiration.

On the third day, he finished, and we made love to commemorate his awakening. Afterward, he held me in his arms.

"I'd like to take you to meet my father tomorrow. We can go to his office for lunch."

"Tomorrow?" I asked. "I have so much to *do*."

"I want him to meet you before the move, so he knows we're doing the right thing. You never know, we may need his help at some point, and I want him to see we're serious about each other."

The man of my dreams wanted me to meet his family because we were so serious. Sounded good to me. "I can't wait." I kissed him before drifting off to sleep.

As I mentioned earlier, Adam's father was a Persian rug dealer. When we arrived at his office, I was shaking with anticipation. Adam behaved very differently with his father than with his mother. Something about his regal Iranian heritage commanded Adam's respect. We entered a wide room lit only by sunlight coming from two windows, with several rolled-up carpets scattered around us. His father was sitting at a small, wooden table, smoking a Marlboro Red with another man, his business partner. I felt their eyes upon me the second I entered.

"Dad," said Adam, "this is Amanda."

"Nice to meet you," I said as I approached. He turned his head slightly to allow me a kiss on his cheek. I took it as a positive sign.

"Nice to meet you," he replied. He spoke with a thick, Middle Eastern accent. "My name is Arnon."

He had a small, lean frame with worn skin, and looked much older than he was. He smoked two packs of cigarettes a day and barely ate, yet conveyed the presence of an ox. While the men made small talk, I remained quiet for the most part as I took it all in.

"I started drawing again," Adam told his father. Arnon remained still, as if he didn't want to admit he had heard correctly. Adam added, "I did a drawing of Amanda. She's my muse."

I smiled shyly. Arnon grunted and glanced in my direction.

"It came out amazing!" I said. "Adam's so gifted."

"Mm-hmm," said Arnon. He turned to Adam. "Why you messing with dat shit again? It's no good for you. It no help you."

"Dad," interrupted Adam, "please stop. I'm fine."

The air grew awkwardly hushed. Adam turned toward a small office across the room and beckoned for me to see something. There on the wall was a framed picture of Adam, shaking Bill Clinton's hand, taken when he won his art award in high school.

"Wow, look at you!" I commented.

He smiled. "I told you I had long hair once."

He wasn't kidding. A thick mane of long, dark hair hung over his shoulders, and he instantly resembled the cover of a romance novel.

"I think, if I knew you in high school, I would've been pregnant before college," I teased.

"I love you," said Adam. "You make me feel so good about myself."

Arnon came up to us and interrupted our googly-eyed stare. Adam recognized it as his queue to leave.

But Arnon needed a moment with me alone first. "You love my son?" he asked.

"Very much," I replied.

"Do you know everything?"

What a strange question. I had known his son for four years. I was moving in with him! Of course I knew everything. "Yes," I answered confidently. "I know *everything.*"

"Very well then." Arnon kissed me on the cheek.

I took it as his seal of approval.

"Take my number," he said. "Just in case."

"Thank you." It felt so nice to have a dad again, to call if we needed anything.

"He liked you," said Adam as we left.

"Think so?"

"I *know* so," he smiled.

I spent the rest of the day packing and painting, barely making a dent on the walls. Adam planned to come over early the next day with his friend Nick to pack up the U-Haul and bring me to our new home. They arrived early, as planned, and Adam was a man on a mission.

"If there's one thing I know," he told me, "it's moving, packing, and loading. Do what I say when I say it, and don't argue. This will go very smoothly if you follow my lead."

Very smoothly meant on Adam's terms. He barked orders throughout the day, took breaks at his pace, and if I remotely disagreed, he jumped down my throat and told me not to battle him. Several hours later, the van was packed and the boys went to Brooklyn while I stayed to finish painting; with everything gone but the cats, it would be easy to complete.

I'm the type of person who likes to finish a task once I start it, especially if it's one I hate, like moving. I can't fully rest leaving things in limbo. Adam returned to my apartment after he dropped off Nick, exhausted. I had finished most of the bedroom and still had half the kitchen left. It had been a twelve-hour day, but it was still only 9:00 p.m. I had enough strength and time to finish, but Adam was done, which meant, apparently, so was I. "Let's go, Amanda! You can finish tomorrow."

"Adam, I'm almost done! It's supposed to be done by *tomorrow*," I insisted.

"By the *end of the day* tomorrow. Come on! I'm tired, and I want to go home."

"I can't stop before I finish. Why don't you take the train back, and I'll stay with the van and head over when I finish?"

"*Listen* to me!" he shouted. "My friend and I just busted our *ass* to move *your shit* into my apartment. He has a bad back and carried your stuff up *two flights of stairs!* We are *done* for today. You are coming home with me *now*, so get your shit and *let's go!* Do not *fight* me. I'll be in the van." He stormed out.

Cold feet left me frozen. If there was ever a *Choose Your Own Adventure* moment, that moment was it. The little girl my parents had raised shouted from within, urged me to be sure I was doing the right thing.

It wasn't too late. I still had the apartment. I could tell my landlord I'd changed my mind. My eyes surveyed the bare room, covered in splotches of white paint, a dead cockroach carcass in the corner. My TV was sold, my bed and all of my belongings gone. Two years of my life spent waiting to live with Adam—and just before it happened, I had witnessed a rage in him I'd never seen before, over something petty and mundane. It's typical of me to call it a sign, uncharacteristic of me not to heed the warning. He was tired, hungry. We all get cranky under those conditions, not to mention we were embarking on a life-altering step with the weight of the world on his shoulders. Perhaps I wasn't being understanding. Perhaps my control issues were less important than conceding to Adam's wishes. Still. . .weren't most couples supposed to be *happy* the night before they moved in together? Shouldn't this be a *joyous* occasion? Were things moving too quickly in the wrong direction, or was a lover's quarrel at a stressful time a silly reason to throw away years of effort? Not knowing how, I had arrived at a crossroads with no clue what to do.

Amanda K. Hirsch

CHAPTER 10

❖

EVER WONDER HOW MANY MARRIAGES end in divorce because the bride or groom is too afraid to call it off at the last minute? Consider the expenses alone: event space, caterers, DJ, flowers, photographer. . .it's endless!

Then there's the embarrassment factor. You're surrounded by dozens of your closest friends and family about to celebrate an important rite of passage, and instead you need to tell them you made a *mistake?*

And let's not forget the emotional cost to your fiancé. That's a whole mess of hurt waiting in the wings. I can absolutely understand people who silence their gut when it grumbles before taking a major relation-ship step.

However, ask any divorcée or bitter breakup survivor who ignored the grumble, and I'm sure they will agree: No amount of money, em-barrassment, or hurt feelings exceeds the level of pain and destruction permanently attached to the wrong relationship.

Divorce can be so expensive both financially and emotionally, there are people who choose murder instead. *Embarrassment?* Who wants to tell their Facebook friends, who '*liked*' all the happy little pictures of their happy little family, that it was all an illusion? After the bitterness of re-

LOVING ADAM

sentment builds up over the years, you long for the days of hurt feelings that healed with a bit of time.

By the end of it, it's the *time* you spent that you can never get back you think about the most. You tell yourself it's not a waste; it helped make you who you are. *What doesn't kill us makes us stronger.* If you have kids, you see them as a blessing and set your pain aside for their sake. But somewhere deep down inside, perhaps late at night when it's just you and your reflection in the bathroom mirror, you wonder. You can't help but imagine what might have been if you'd only listened to your gut way back when. You think about whatever superficial cost kept you from abandoning the wrong relationship, and you laugh at the smallness of it compare to the value of the time you threw away. You think about starting over and what it will take.

For some, all this is too much and they choose to stay. Some people feel it's better to have someone than no one. Those folks may not end up alone, but they often end up lonely, even with a partner at their side.

Many years ago, my friend Tally and I came up with a homemade adage: *Be careful whom you try to squeeze into your picture.* We coined this phrase after I invited her one night, at Happy Hour, to secretly meet a work crush of mine. She spent ten minutes talking to him and told me I was insane.

Your *picture* is an imaginary snapshot of your life at any given moment in time. It represents a lens of focus that narrowly constricts your world view to only what you can see and fit in to your frame. The work crush Tally met was fairly bland and not my type, but since he was the only young, single guy in my field of view, I made him out to be far more than he was.

The cool thing about our gut is that it sees the big picture when the flash from our snapshot blinds us. Our willingness to listen when our gut speaks defines our future.

That night, as Adam waited for me in the van and I scanned the bare

| 79 |

walls that surrounded me, my unwillingness to hear my gut, and my failure to see the big picture, defined me. I gathered the cats, shut off the lights, and chose Brooklyn with Adam instead.

There were brief moments, scattered over the next two weeks, when I can remember feeling happy. Flashes of laughter and peace intermingled with spurts of excitement over our new beginning. They served as a weak glue that bonded cracks I couldn't, or *wouldn't,* see.

Adam was still reading the alien books and studying Freemasonry. I may have been the inspiration for his first work of art to get his feet wet, but he dove in head first by way of a six-by-nine-foot canvas on which he planned to artistically capture the essence of religion, Freemasonry, and ancient alien history, using mounds of information and symbolism he had jammed into his head the previous few months.

Words cannot accurately describe the magnitude of this piece of work. Detailed faces represented ancient gods, a self-portrait of Adam, old and haggard, among them. Geometric symbols and angles appeared everywhere in bright, bold colors. He had a vision that could easily translate to a semester's worth of graduate-level information on all related subject matter, the teacher in him unleashed. Truth be told, I couldn't look at the painting for more than a few minutes at a time. It made me physically ill. It worsened the more Adam talked about it. Soon, it was *all* he talked about. Every free moment was spent working on the painting, and each night, he got less and less sleep.

In the meantime, he got involved in a real estate project that meant working closely with a rabbi and members of a nearby temple. I remind you, Adam's mother is Jewish; his father is Muslim. Adam was not religious by any means. He used what he knew from both cultures to work with people from the same background, but the extent of his belief was a Higher Power of his own interpretation. After meeting the rabbi, he began acting strangely. On Friday, July 11, he attended Shabbat dinner at the rabbi's home to celebrate the Sabbath. When he returned, he was wearing a yarmulke and spoke of a new kinship towards his people. His eyes welled up as he spoke.

"Hon? What is it?" I asked.

"It's just all so beautiful," he said.

He'd cried more times than I could count over the past few weeks. He claimed he'd had to hold back his emotions over the years so he wouldn't seem like less of a man. I apparently made him feel comfortable enough to let me see the real him. The real him cried. . .*a lot.*

In addition to the recent increase in his emotions came an equal surge in his sex drive. Making love felt more methodical than passionate. We mentally connected less, while Adam moved faster and harder inside me than he used to. That night, his hands started out soft on my body, and I thought I might finally taste a bit of tenderness.

He whispered in my ear, "So. . .we live together now, you know what that means?"

"What, baby?"

"Time for anal."

"What did you say?" I gasped. *So much for tenderness.*

"Anal sex." He was dead serious. "You said you would do it with me when we moved in together."

"I did *not!*" I snapped.

"Oh, come on. You did, too."

I have no desire whatsoever to have anal sex. If I go my whole life without that experience, it's fine by me. That said, I believe in monogamy and the need to spice things up at times. If *anal* was destined to become part of my sexual ars-*enal*, it would be with my husband, hopefully several years into our marriage. I'd established this personal creed long before I met Adam, and there was no chance of him convincing me otherwise. "Adam, I said I would do that with you if we got married. Not just living together."

"You're such a liar!" he teased.

"No, I'm not."

"I'll show you what I do to liars."

Before I knew it, I was face down on the bed with him behind me. He grabbed my pants and jerked them to my knees, my bare ass exposed to the air. For a split second, in the depth of my core, I didn't know what would happen next. The Adam I knew would never hurt me, but he also wouldn't joke like this.

I screamed, "Adam, *stop*!"

"Oh, my God, are you okay?" he asked, worried.

"What the fuck is *wrong* with you?" I yelled.

"I was just *kidding*. I wasn't gonna *do* anything."

"Well, it wasn't fucking funny." I got up and went to the bathroom frustrated by yet another unseen side of Adam.

When I returned, Adam had softened to his former self. He apologized profusely and handled me with the care I deserved. Before long, he was inside me and made me scream. Seconds later, he left me alone in the bed to go paint. It was late, and I was too tired to fight. I had to work the next day.

Work always helped take my mind off things. I didn't exactly enjoy being an operations manager at a tourist attraction, in fact I rather hated the work itself, but I loved the people I worked with. To this day, I consider most of them friends. Without their laughter and support, I'm not sure I would've survived the events that would soon take place.

When I got home Saturday evening, Adam had Wu Tang Clan playing loudly on the stereo as he painted. He didn't notice I had entered the room until I turned down the music.

"You're here!" he said excitedly. "Come see what I've done to the piece."

Under my breath, I mocked, "*Hi, honey, how was your day? Mine was fine, thank you for asking.*"

My sarcasm blew past him.

"Sit here." He moved a chair in front of the canvas. "Tell me what you see."

I saw a fucking mess. Granted, components of the mess were technically magnificent and indicative of Adam's skill as an artist, but the layout made me sick. I'm sure it made sense to him at the time, and if you asked him today he could probably still give you a clear lesson on the material. I'm no Presidential scholar, but I saw the mess of his mind translated into a jumbled mass of color and shape on canvas.

"Adam, I just got home. I don't want to look at the painting right now. I want to relax and unwind." Since I didn't know how to address the underlying situation, I avoided it.

"Oh, okay. Later, then." He followed me to the bedroom. "We have to record *Ancient Aliens* tonight, they have this great special on—"

"Adam, *stop!* I don't want to hear about aliens or Masons or anything like that. I just want to chill. Is that possible?"

"Sure, gorgeous," he answered sweetly. He hadn't called me that in weeks.

"Thank you," I sighed.

"Let's order dinner. Do you think you could work on my back a little bit afterwards?" he asked.

At the time I didn't care that Adam made everything about him. I wanted him to stop talking. "I'll massage your back, but *after* dinner. For now I want some peace."

Shortly before the move, he had begun complaining of a chronic pain in his ribcage when he moved or took a deep breath. After a night in the emergency room during which doctors took X-Rays and a series of tests, they told us he had sprained the intercostal muscle on his right side, probably due to severe coughing. He'd had a recent bout with bronchitis, and he smoked enough to conceive he had strained something. The doctors prescribed Vicodin to help with the pain. *(Cue ominous music.)*

After dinner, he lay face down on the floor. "Push hard," he said. "I can take it."

"I don't want to press too hard. If it's sprained, I'll make it worse."

"You won't make it worse! Don't battle me. Just press hard, use your elbow."

I did as I was told.

"Harder!" he cried out.

"I'm pressing as hard as I can!" I shouted.

"Stand on me."

"Adam, no! I'll crush you!"

"Stand on me, you won't crush me. I need to *release the pain!*"

"Fine!" Moving delicately, I stood on his back while he emitted sounds of painful satisfaction.

"Oh, thank you, Amanda. That was wonderful. It helped so much." He leaped up off the ground. "I'm a new man!" He kissed me on the cheek and went to paint.

As I write, I get annoyed just thinking about it. That night, however, I welcomed his distraction. If painting kept him at bay, I wanted him to paint his little heart out. I don't remember him coming to bed, but I clearly remember the peaceful look on his face as he slept when I left for work Sunday morning. Hooker was curled up on his chest, and for the first time in a long while, Adam was totally quiet. I smiled at the Kodak moment that reminded me why I was there to begin with.

At four o'clock that afternoon, I called to see if he needed anything on my way home. He told me his stepmother and stepsister were headed over for a visit. They wanted to meet me, and he wanted to show them his art. I cringed momentarily.

"They're coming *today*?" I exclaimed.

"Yeah, you'll probably get here around the same time as them."

"Adam, the house is a mess. I've worked all day. This isn't how I wanted to meet them for the first time. We were going to have them over for dinner."

"Oh, stop, it's fine. My dad called a little while ago. He said Pilar and Ana wanted to come meet you. I couldn't just say no."

"Fine. Do we need anything?"

"No, just hurry up and get here."

So little went according to my plans in those days that I chose to roll with it. I had been desperate for any scrap of conventional living since our move. For an evening, we would be a happy couple entertaining in our new home. I reached the apartment seconds after the women. Adam met them at the front door as I came up the walkway. He wore a black piece of cloth tied on his head like the *keffiyeh* Arab men wear.

He saw me approach. "Here she is!"

The two ladies greeted me with warm hugs that instantly put me at ease. I'd had concerns, knowing how they had felt about Beth, but neither of them ever made it an issue. Ana was barely twenty-one and adorable. She spoke about Adam like a little sister about a big brother, though they hadn't spent much time together growing up.

We made our way inside, and Adam showed them the painting while I put away my things.

After a few minutes, Pilar sat with me on the couch while Ana and Adam caught up in the kitchen. She made small talk with questions about my work and family as we watched the other two from a distance. Adam was more animated than ever.

"That's some painting," said Pilar. I saw a change in her face I couldn't recognize.

"It sure is," I agreed. "He's very talented."

"Is he sleeping?" she asked.

"Not as much as he used to. He stays up late to paint."

"Make sure he gets rest." She rose from the couch. "C'mon, Ana, we need to get going."

"You're leaving *already?*" asked Adam.

"Yes, it's been a long day, and we need to get home." Ana looked surprised but followed her mother's lead.

Adam and I walked them to their car to exchange goodbyes. Pilar hugged me tight. "Amanda, it's been lovely to meet you. Hang in there, and we'll see you again soon." She gave Adam a hug and whispered something in his ear I couldn't make out.

Ana hugged me good-bye. "Please take care of my brother."

"I promise," I smiled.

"Take my cell number, just in case you need to reach us for anything," said Ana.

Adam bounced from the car to the front door and up the stairs to the apartment. Energy oozed off him like cartoon puffs of smoke. I stayed to watch the women disappear out of sight up the street. I kept thinking of the look on Pilar's face when we were on the couch—as if she knew something she wasn't telling me. Her hasty departure made me wonder.

I'm sure, if you counted all the brief seconds of doubt or concern that passed through me over the course of months leading up to this moment, there would be enough hours that, had I felt them all at once, they might have had an impact. But subtle pangs weigh nothing compared to the power of love mixed with lust and ego. When I returned to the apartment, I was rudely awakened.

Hip-Hop was blaring again through the walls when I reached the third floor, a few feet from our door. I rolled my eyes and went in. The living room was empty. To my left, I saw Adam standing in the kitchen before his painting. His arms were spread wide, his head, still wrapped in the scarf, tilted up towards the ceiling with his eyes closed. My mouth dropped. I had no idea what he was doing and I didn't want to find out. I turned off the music.

He jolted out of his trance. "What are you doing?" he asked angrily.

"It's really loud, Adam. The neighbors are going to complain."

I went to the bedroom to change clothes. A mound of junk was piled on top of the dresser. As I stood there in my bra and underwear, I suddenly felt Adam's hands on my waist. I turned to face him and finally asked, "Are you feeling okay?"

He looked at me with a huge smile. "I'm better than okay," he said. "*I'm awake.*"

Suddenly, Cleopatra fell off the top of the dresser. I didn't realize she had buried herself in the junk. On the way down, she scratched my left leg.

I cried out in pain.

"Cleo, bad girl!" Adam barked. "Come here," he said to me, and guided me over to the bed to sit down and assess the scratch.

"It's my fault," I said. "I didn't see her there. I don't even know what startled her."

He smiled deviously. "You are like me, Amanda. Now that I am awake, you too will soon be awake. You'll see, when that happens, the Universe starts to react. You'll notice a lot of these random scratches and bruises while it tries to knock you off your path." He left to get me a Band-Aid.

I scanned my body and suddenly noticed random scratches and bruises all down my left side. I had one on my arm and foot from the move, and a scratch on my nipple I couldn't explain. Now, as if the Universe had thrown Cleo at me, my shin was bleeding. For a moment, in my head, I heard *Twilight Zone* music. *Is Adam onto something?* I wondered. The real question should have been, *What something is Adam on?* It might have saved me a few headaches.

When he returned, I changed tactics. Since he kept saying he was able to be himself around me, I figured I'd share a new side of me in return.

"Adam," I asked, "have you ever noticed I don't sing in front of you?"

"Not particularly."

"Well, I'm not sure you're aware of it, but I *love* to sing. When we worked at the gym, you used to tease us when we sang along with the music, so I've kind of held back ever since." I left out the part about feeling inferior to Beth, a classically trained opera singer.

"You don't have to hold back." He smiled. "You can sing whenever you want."

"I'd like to sing for you now." I had spent the last few days learning a Fiona Apple song I planned to show off with.

"Okay," said Adam.

I retrieved my MP3 player and had proceeded to queue my music when Adam instantly stood up and went to the kitchen.

"Where are you going?" I asked confused.

"To call my Mom."

Huh? There I am, about to press play and reveal a rather personal side of myself, when Adam suddenly gets the urge to call his mother? He couldn't wait another two minutes, after I spent weeks revolved around his *awakening?* I was embarrassed and annoyed, to say the least. If I had a do-over, I would let it go. I would patiently wait until Adam ended his phone call with his mother and I had his full attention. I *wouldn't* be a petty smart-ass. Instead, I chose to sing. I put on my headphones and belted Fiona from the bedroom.

There was a moment of quiet when I finished the song, before Adam came rushing in enraged: a silence that signaled the death of my life, as I knew it. The man who left the room to call his mother had returned a *Pet Sematary* version of the Adam I had known for four years.

CHAPTER 11

❖

ADAM CAME AT ME FROM THE KITCHEN. He moved fast, with purpose. Right around the halfway point, he failed to slow down, and I saw a look in his eye. I backed up against the bed, startled by his pace. He stopped an inch from my face and peered down at me. "What the *fuck* is your problem?" he demanded.

I tried to play dumb. "What?"

"I'm on the phone with my mother, who has fucking *cancer*, and you're in here yelling at the top of your lungs? Who the fuck do you think you are?"

I kept expecting him to calm down, but he didn't.

"*Answer* me!" Adam yelled. "Who the *fuck* do you think you *are?*"

Had I managed to mentally process the irrational turn things had taken, I might have backed down and tried to handle the situation with care. Instead, the Puerto Rican female in me took over, and I tried to defend myself. I didn't realize a switch had flipped in Adam, that there was never anything I could do to stop it.

"Adam, I finally open up to you about my singing and you get up and walk away!"

"Oh, please! You're singing. . .you're *singing*. You're a spoiled little piggy crying about her singing. *Wah-wah.*"

Whoa. This was not a reaction I understood. *Did he call me piggy? Is he calling me fat?*

I took the poisoned bait. "Fuck you, Adam!"

He smirked with pleasure at my anger. That's when it became clear I was dealing with a different Adam than I knew. The eerie smile wasn't his. It was coming from someone, or *something*, else, I realized. Without meaning to, I revealed my fear. He sensed my weakness and pounced.

"What's the matter? The spoiled, little piggy upset she didn't get her way?" He shook his finger in my face as he spoke. "You're a fucking *piggy!* I've fucking *had* it with you! How dare you come in to my house and fucking try to disrespect me! You fucking piggy."

Physically, I froze. I felt my soul slip out of my body and scan the room for exits, hidden cameras, anything that might help me comprehend what was happening and how to handle it. He darted through the apartment. He slipped through every room, moving non-stop, cursing me out with profanity and insults that cut to the core.

"Adam, please stop!" I thought I might throw up.

"Stop? Stop what, piggy? Stop telling you the truth? That you're a fucking psycho, wild banshee, and I'm fucking *sick* of you?"

My face must have said it all, because I couldn't find the words.

"Yup, that's right," he went on. "I want you out of my fucking house. *Now!*"

Did he just say he wants me out? "Adam, I'm not leaving."

"Oh, yes you are, piggy!"

"Stop *calling* me that!" I screamed.

"But that's what you *are.* A fucking little piggy. And you will leave this house. This is *my* house. *I'm* on the fucking lease, and I will call the cops and have you arrested for trespassing!"

"Adam!" I cried, "I can't leave. I have nowhere to go!"

"Fine, you fucking banshee. *I'll* leave."

"No, Adam, don't go!" I blocked the door. Maybe if we could each take a breath, we could talk it out.

"Get out of my way!" he yelled.

"No!" I yelled back.

He grabbed my Blackberry and ran to the window. "If you don't let me leave, I will drop this right now!"

"Adam, that's my *work* phone!"

"I'm counting to three. One. . .two—"

"Fine!" I yelled, and stepped aside. He tossed my phone on the couch and bolted out the door.

If this ever happens to you, call the police. Easier said than done. When he left, calling the police didn't even cross my mind. Shocked beyond belief, utterly confused, I sank onto the bed, feeling numb. How had my effort to sing a song led to being called a "piggy" and a "banshee" and being kicked out of the house?

I blamed myself. My childish efforts to intentionally annoy him during his phone call reflected my knack for occasionally taking things too far. It had been selfish of me to demand attention over his cancer-stricken mother. I took the fault for the events that had taken place, because my rational mind was struggling to make rational sense of a completely irrational situation. It wasn't until much later that I realized a million tiny triggers could have set Adam off that night, and probably had. My behavior, while immature and guilty of bad timing, hadn't merited his reaction.

That night, when I thought about him kicking me out of the house, I ultimately ignored it. He knew I had nowhere to go, and even if he wanted to break up with me, he'd never kick me out on the street. That just wouldn't happen. When I replayed his insults in my head, I skipped through them like dead air. Why? Because none of it made sense! None of it *fit*. He didn't use words like "piggy" and "banshee," let alone use them towards me. It was like listening to another language: You hear the sounds, but you tune them out because you simply don't understand them. Surviving meant taking the blame for our lover's quarrel and getting past something that had started out being so trivial. When Adam returned, I would apologize, we would make up, and all would be well.

He answered his cell when I tried him shortly after he left. He said, since I wouldn't leave the apartment, I needed to leave him alone, that he would be back when he felt like it. I chose not to poke the bear in the zoo and let him be.

After a couple of hours, the clock approached midnight, and he was still not home and had stopped answering my calls. My alarm was set to ring at 5:00 a.m. for an opening shift the next day. As I lay there in the dark, the fog of my rational guilt began to lift, and more than anything I wished I could leave the house, exactly as he asked me to. I wished him to come home and find me gone, but that seemed impossible with only $1.59 in my bank account until my direct deposit hit in a few hours. My family was already worried about me 24/7; a late-night phone call would have done, I told myself, more harm than good. In my head, I couldn't face any of the friends I had just told about our fairy tale love story without looking like a total idiot, and I would never leave Oliver and Lulu behind.

In flashes, I started to piece together the past few months, connected the dots between Adam's particularly bizarre behaviors the last two weeks. I recalled Arnon asking, "Do you know everything?" and Pilar's creepy expression I couldn't quite place. I thought of Ana...*That's it!* Ana! She had given me her number "just in case."

By then, it felt too late to call, and I didn't want to worry Ana if it turned out to be nothing. My fog of fault may have lifted, but the denial of it all stuck to me like early morning dew. I quickly typed out a text:

Ana, it's Amanda! Ur brother and I had a fight. He kicked me out of the house and left. He's still not home. I'm sorry, I don't know what to do. Can I have ur dad's number or can u have him call me ASAP??? Thx!

Somewhere between my worry, confusion and fear, I managed to fall asleep as I prayed for her response. At around 2:30 a.m., the jiggle of keys in the front door woke me up. I had kept my eyes closed, pretending to be asleep, when I suddenly felt Adam hover over me.

"No, I don't think so. *Wake up!*" he barked.

"Adam?" I expected a demon voice to tell me he no longer lived there.

"Who the fuck else would it be? Get up. If you won't fucking leave, there's no way you're fucking sleeping in my bed." He took the covers off me.

"I need to be up in two hours, Adam. Can't I just sleep here? I won't bother you."

"No, you won't bother me. You can never bother me, you fucking little piggy. You know why? Because you are nothing compared to me. You're a filthy, spoiled piggy. I. . .am up here!" He held his hand high in the air. "You. . .are down here." He lowered his hand equally low.

A deep sigh escaped me. Adam had been gone for hours, but instead of cooling off, he was amped up and angry. I gave in to the surreal nightmare I found myself in. If time apart had only made things worse, nothing I could say or do would help. I simply needed to survive the night and get to work the next day. Then I would call my sister, and she would tell me what to do. It was only a couple of hours. If I left him alone, he would likely do the same. *Yeah. . .right.*

Conceding the fight, I moved towards the black leather couch in the living room.

"That's right piggy, go. And take your filthy fucking cats with you. Look at them!" He was speaking with vehemence. "Look at Lulu, look at how you take care of her. She's fucking so fat she can't walk. Her skin is all flaky. You shouldn't be allowed to have cats."

It was as if he kept closets full of my skeletons buried away in his mind, and the monster invading his body could unlock them to use as ammo. He stomped through the house like a madman, ranting and raving about me. I remained quiet on the couch, eyes closed, hoping the sun would rise soon and I could be on my way. I was physically drained and prayed for him to stop talking. As desperate as I was for sleep, I didn't feel safe sleeping with him still awake.

He came and sat in the chair next to me to roll a blunt, muttering insults and adding to injury. "Fucking gave up my marriage for a fucking little piggy. A selfish, little piggy," he mumbled.

I'm pretty sure I was only managing to stay quiet and ignore him out of fear. Instantly, his voice grew loud.

"Where is my *weed?* You fucking *stole my weed!* You fucking piggy, you *stole my weed.*" He was screaming as if I were part of a conspiracy.
"I didn't touch your weed!" I said frantically. "I haven't seen your weed since right after Pilar left!"

"You're a fucking *liar.* You hid it from me cause you're a selfish, filthy piggy!" As he screamed this again, he pushed my forehead with his index finger: "Give me my fucking *weed!*"

The reality was that Adam had taken his weed with him when he left. He'd been more amped up when he returned because, when he left, he'd gone on the hunt for cocaine and spent his hours getting high while I was home blaming myself for his behavior. Somewhere along the way, he had forgotten what happened to his weed, and it'd become my fault.

So far in these pages, I have described my love for Adam in great detail, in the hope of making you understand that only a love that deep could have blinded me to the course of events so obviously building up over time.

Yet that night, entangled in my web of love for him, I saw how quickly love can turn to hate and make a person snap. When I felt him press his finger against my forehead, I briefly understood how a decent, rational human being could commit murder. I didn't think about how he was enraged, drugged, and so outside his mind he could kill me. I didn't pause to try to swallow my pride until the sun came up. I didn't think. I *reacted*.

"Don't fucking *touch* me!" I jumped up off the couch, pushing him away.

"You *see?*" he screamed. "You're a fucking *banshee!* A fucking *chupacabra!*" He literally snarled and growled. With his face framed by the *keffiyeh*, he resembled a rabid Sphinx.

Instantly I regained my senses and tried to reason with him. "Adam, *please!* I love you! Just calm down." We stood a few feet apart, almost waiting in anticipation.

"Fucking *calm down?* You *beat* me! That's right! I have pictures of the bruises from you *beating* me!"

I didn't know what he was talking about until he gripped the spot on his back he had made me massage and stand on the night before. If there was a bruise, it was because he'd asked for it, but I knew, seen from another angle, how it could look bad.

"Yes, filthy piggy. You beat me, and you held a *knife* to me!" he cried. "I will tell everyone about you, and you will go to jail. You'll spend your life in a cage like the animal you are!" He drew back his hand as if he was casting an imaginary ball of fire in my direction, his eyes wide with fury.

He looked so ridiculous it made me chuckle nervously and mimic him with my own flame. When I pulled back my hand the way he had, he freaked. To this day, I truly believe he saw a flame. It reminded me of the movie *Batman Begins*. The villain doses his victims with a hallucinogenic powder that makes them think they're seeing a monster when it's only an average person in real life.

Adam flew back in retreat and fell onto a chair. When I took a step towards him to see if he was okay, he kicked me in the stomach to get me away from him and knocked me on my ass. I rapidly pulled myself together and caught my breath. If I wasn't careful, there was no telling where this would go.

"I'm sorry," I said as I stood up slowly. "I didn't mean to scare you." He watched me in terror, defensively awaiting my next move. I was spent. I had no more energy. It was 4:45 a.m., and I needed to get ready for work. I turned toward the bedroom.

"Where do you think you're going?" he asked as though I required his permission.

"To get my clothes to bring to the bathroom. I open today, and I need to get to work. They'll worry if I don't show up."

"They wouldn't worry if they knew how much you hated working there," he growled. "I'm the only fucking reason you're even still there." He followed me from the dresser to the closet, back through the living room and kitchen, to the bathroom. "You're a stupid piggy who wanted to quit, but I gave you the confidence to stay. You owe that job to me!" He blocked the bathroom door and held his finger centimeters from my head.

I looked at his finger.

"What, woman? I'm not touching you. Not like you, who fucking *beat* me." He thoroughly enjoyed threatening and manipulating me without physically putting a finger on me. "Woman. That's right, *wo-man*. You know what's in there? *Man*. That means you are nothing without me, *man*. Even your name—" his finger was now almost blinding one eye— "A-*man*-da. In it is *man* and *Adam*. You are *nothing* without me."

"You're right, Adam," I said. "I'm nothing without you. My work, everything. . .I owe it all to you."

"That's fucking right," he answered.

"Please, Adam," I begged, "let me get ready for work. I can't be late."

Perhaps it was that I agreed with him, or that, as dawn approached, the soul-sucking vampire in him grew weary. He lowered his finger and stepped aside as if it was an act of mercy. After twelve hours in overdrive, he started to settle down. A look of exhaustion swept over his face, and he zombie-walked towards the bedroom.

I closed the bathroom door and found Lulu and Oliver huddled together in a corner. They must have taken shelter from the chaos I had subjected them to. With the sound of the shower to drown out the sounds of my tears, as it had for Beth many months before, I fell to the floor and lay down before their furry, little paws. Oliver bumped my head with his to tell me things would be okay.

Those four walls seemed to protect me; I didn't leave the bathroom until I was absolutely ready to go to work. I was nervous leaving my cats, but despite Adam's turn against me, I couldn't imagine him hurting an innocent animal. The fact I even had to wonder boggled my mind.

I managed to leave the house successfully without waking Adam. On the train ride in, I caught a glimpse of myself in the glass. Circles of pain and fatigue framed my eyes, tinted red and swollen from crying. The night's events looped through my mind with worse thoughts of what would happen when I went back later in the day. Along the walk to my office, it hit me that I had given up everything to be with a monster. My co-worker, Kevin, showed up while I was going robotically through the motions to prepare for the day. He took one look at me and asked what had happened. I broke down in tears and told him how my boyfriend had morphed into a crazy man and kicked me out of the house.

Poor Kevin had no idea what he'd walked in to, but he handled it like a champ. He sat next to me and said very quietly, "Amanda, calm down. Sit here, and I'll take care of the morning meeting. When Greg comes in, explain to him what's going on. I'm sure he'll let you go figure this all out."

Kevin was right. When my boss Greg arrived, he listened to me recount a summary of my horror story. I was so tired I couldn't control the sobs between sentences. He told me not to worry, that everything would work out. He excused me for the day, and with the next two days off, I'd have a chance to get my ducks in a row.

In a complete daze I left the building and was two blocks south before I finally called my sister, Debbie. As a second mother and best
friend, she could always talk me off a ledge and ease the stress of any situation. "Deb, I don't know what to do. It's like I don't even know him!"
I cried. "He's not the same person."

"Listen to me," she said calmly. "Here's what you're gonna do. You're
going to come home and get the car. Then you're going to go back to
Brooklyn, pack a bag, pick up the cats, and come stay with us for a couple
of weeks while you work things out."

I sobbed, "Okay."

She went on, "Lots of couples panic when they first move in together. You probably just need some time apart to cool off and clear
your heads so you can work it out."

"I think Adam hates me."

"He doesn't hate you," she said. "He just left his wife for you! Whatever's going on, you'll figure it out, but for now you need to come home.
Look at it as a summer vacation."

". . .Okay," I said. "I'll head straight to the bus now."

"Call me when you get here, and I'll take you to get Mom's car.
Don't worry, I'll fill her in on what's going on."

My sister had an exceptional talent for creating perspective.   I
hung up and gazed at the city surrounding me. I felt like Alice down
the rabbit hole after a swig from the *Drink Me* bottle, tiny in a giant world
that seemed to change overnight.

CHAPTER 12

❖

I T AMAZES ME THE LENGTHS the Universe will go to steer you in a certain direction. Equally awe-inspiring is the persistence of human nature to ignore it by choice. Somehow I made it home safely to get my mom's car and back to Brooklyn without a word from Adam. As far as I knew, he was still asleep where I left him. I even imagined somehow that, when he woke up, the whole thing would be my dream.

A pit started to build in my gut as I climbed the two flights of stairs. There was no sound coming from any of the apartments. It was an early Monday afternoon. Surely, everyone was at work. Or perhaps they heard the ruckus the night before and pretended to be asleep the way I had the last time I heard footsteps approach.

Before I unlocked the door, I took a deep, calming breath and told myself to shake it off. There was always the chance I'd go inside and Adam would be back to his charming self, smitten with me and in love. Maybe I'd open the door to an apology spelled out in rose petals, and we could move on from our first fight as a live-in couple. Wasn't the key to destroying Freddie Krueger's power to realize the monster wasn't real? The problem was that I was comparing Adam to Freddie Krueger in the first place.

The bed was unmade but empty. I called out for Adam as I cleared the other rooms but saw no sign of him. A noise from the closet made me wobble for a second where I stood. Oliver came running out at the sound of my voice, thankful for my rescue. I sat down for a brief moment and said a silent prayer of thanks, never more grateful to be alone. Once done, I quickly packed a bag for my escape. It took two trips to load the car. I managed to complete the task in under an hour, but the closer I came to freedom, the more my heart pounded that Adam might show up. God only knew what would happen then.

After a virtual sprint the last few steps to the car, I started the engine and moved a safe distance down the street in case Adam returned. The time had come to tell him my plans. Each ring of his cell felt like bullets in a game of Russian roulette. When he answered, I paused in fear the phone might explode.

"Yes?" he answered coldly.

"Adam, it's me." I spoke in a soft, calm tone to convey apology and forgiveness. "I'm gonna be staying with my family a couple of weeks while we sort things out. I have Lulu and Ollie with me."

"You owe me six hundred dollars for rent," said Adam.

That was it. That was all he had to say. I couldn't speak.

"I'm coming to your work to pick it up. You did get *paid* today, *didn't you?*" asked Adam.

"Yes, I got paid, but—"

"But nothing. You owe me rent, and I'm coming to get it right now."

"No, you're not. I'm not at work. I already left with the cats."

"Listen to me, you fucking little *piggy!*" he snapped. "You owe me six hundred dollars for rent, and you will pay it or I will have you arrested."

Like putty in his hands, I reacted, "You kicked me out of the house, and now you're asking for a full month of *rent?* I don't think so."

He became infuriated. "Oh, now you're not gonna *pay?* You're a fucking demon, a *chupacabra!* I will fucking come to your work and *make* you pay."

He'd started the game again, but I had neither the energy nor desire to play. "Adam, of course I'm going to give you rent money, but I'm not near the city. It can't be now. Maybe tomorrow."

"Amanda, you will bring me this money *now*. Or else!"

"I'm sorry," I told him, "I can't. Tomorrow, we can meet somewhere by my work and I'll have security escort me out to give it to you." The security threat was bound to set him off, but I hung up before he had a chance to respond. With seat belts fastened, the cats and I made our way to the home I grew up in to take shelter from a romance I had been forced to flee.

When I arrived, my nieces and nephew gave me hugs strong enough to forget my troubles the rest of the day. I turned off my cell to let it rest in the guest room along with my thoughts of Adam. That night, I fell asleep surrounded by the comfort of childhood dreams that had never prepared me for such a nightmare.

Each morning when I open my eyes and realize it's the start of a new day, I feel a moment of peace, timeless seconds that hover in the air between sleep and being awake like a camera lens that struggles to focus. Somewhere in that purgatory between realms, you're able to forget the bad and, for just a moment, take solace in the good.

My family let me sleep in the following morning while they made their way to work and school. My sister and her family had moved in with my mother when my father died of lung cancer in 1999. With three kids in the house under the age twelve, one savored quiet times like this.

As I fully came to, I noticed I left my phone off all night. When it powered up, I saw that Adam had left me a voicemail that woke me up to the new reality I was living in:

"Hey Amanda, it's me. Um. . .I just want to arrange. . .um, a time, 4:00 p.m., to pick up money. Actually, um. . .if there is any security, if I feel there's

a threat, or if I feel there's a threat from someone else, I'll have security there, too. But there won't need to be security if you don't bring security down. You can just come bring my money peacefully. Or actually. . .if you could have one of your co-workers take me upstairs. . .in the nice, pretty elevator. . .so I could have a nice, bird's eye view of the city. And myself. . .in my nice three-piece suit, I'll just come and pick up my six hundred dollars tomorrow. I better not feel threatened, and I better get my money, or else I'll have you arrested for hitting me, because I already took pictures and everything, and went to the cops, and everything. They will fuckin' arrest you, you little fuckin' piggy! If you have security, and if you don't do what I say. . . . Or. . .you could take me up there yourself. I just wanna go up there and have a nice view. And that's it. I'll keep my mouth shut like a good little boy. If you just take me up, you give me what you took from me, because you fuckin' beat me and I'll have you put in jail forever. . . . Forever! They will rape and sodomize you, and make you a little fuckin' dike that you hate. You little lesbian hater, I will fuckin' bury you! Alright? So you just. . . basically, ya know. . .follow the law. Because I just. . .work by the law. No physical threats. So you bring my money, you have me go up to the observation deck, so I can take some pictures and do some drawings like a good little boy, because that's all I wanna do. And. . .I get my money. Or I'll just show up while you're working, anytime. . .ya know, buy a ticket. Because ya know, I could do that whenever I want. Under any name, any passport. . . . And I'll just come up and have you behave like a civil. . . civil little woman, and teach you how to be a human being, you little, fucking . . .savage beast! Alright?"

I turned to the cats, nestled in the blanket next to me. "Ollie, Lulu . . . . We're not in Kansas anymore." Ollie meowed slightly. He obviously agreed. It had been two days since Adam started calling me "piggy." If it had just been a phase, it would've passed by now, I felt. Something was wrong. I called Ana again and left a message of my own.

"Ana, it's Amanda. I'm staying at my mother's right now. Adam left me a voice mail, and I think there may be something really wrong with him. He *really* seems to *hate* me. He's not himself. Could you please have your dad check on him? Thanks."

A few hours went by before I heard anything. I knew *something* was wrong with Adam. I even admitted something wrong had been building for much longer than I realized. But I still didn't know what it was or to what extent he was affected. I thought he was angry with me or changed his mind about loving me. That could be the only explanation, since the truth never occurred to me as an alternative.

Finally, Ana returned my call. "Adam is okay," she said. "He's with Beth."

My heart sank from my chest. ". . .He is?" I felt woozy.

"Yes. He was complaining about some kind of pain in his back, and he called Beth to take him to Emergency because she has their health insurance information."

"Oh." I supposed that made sense.

"Yeah, well, when he got there," said Ana, "I guess they figured out he was having an episode, and they admitted him to the psych ward. He's at New York Presbyterian, the sixth floor."

"An. . .*episode?*"

"Yes," said Ana. "Adam is bipolar. Didn't you know that?"

Did I? "Adam mentioned something happened years ago, but he said he's been off his medication for years, and he was fine."

"Well, he's not fine. He's sick. But don't worry, my dad is with him, and he'll be okay. I'll call you soon with an update."

When we ended the call, I felt my throat close. The room went blurry, and I couldn't breathe. My world was crashing down around me. The man I so deeply loved and sacrificed everything for had just gone running back to his ex-wife in his hour of need.

Can you believe *that* was my main concern? Not the episode, not the hospital. It was the sheer, primal, cat-like response to the news

Adam had reached out for Beth when he was sick. Me? I was a *chupacabra.*

I immediately dialed my sister at work in hysterics and told her what Ana had said.

"You need to *calm down!*" she shouted over my sobs.

"But. . .he chose *Beth!*" I wailed.

"You are missing the point," said Debbie. "Ana just told you the man has bipolar disorder. She told you he is *sick!* Do you *hear* me? Adam is *sick!*"

"Yes, but he should want *me* when he's sick. I want to take care of him."

"Mandy, this is not the kind of sick like when you have a cold or the flu and you want someone you love to take care of you," said my sister. "Adam is not in his right mind. That means it's no longer the Adam you know. That's why he's turning to Beth. *He's insane!*"

"Maybe he just realized he made a mistake and she's really the one he wants," I maintained.

How my sister is able to remain calm in chaotic situations never fails to impress me. "Listen to me, Adam just had an affair with you for two years, divorced his wife, and moved in with you. If he were in his right mind, he would turn to you. This is actually good news."

"*Good news? That's* a half-full mentality if I ever heard one."

"Yes. Think about it. The fact that he's sick tells us he didn't mean all the things he was saying to you or the way he treated you. Who gives a fuck if he went to Beth? He's in the hospital, he'll get his medicine, and once he's right in the head again, he'll be back with you. You'll see."

I gave in to reality. "I guess you're right."

". . .Did you know he was that sick?" she asked.

"No," I replied, ashamed of myself. "I had *no idea.*"

"I wouldn't beat yourself up," said Debbie. "I'm betting he wanted it that way."

CHAPTER 13

❖

HAVE I MENTIONED YET that I have two tattoos? One is in Chinese lettering and means "*Live for today.*" The other is of a Phoenix. In Harry Potter, they mention three traits of the mythical bird that prompted me to mark myself with its symbol. The Phoenix can carry tremendously heavy burdens; their tears have healing powers; and, when they die, they burst into flames and are reborn from their ashes.

While this may reveal a level of insight into my personality, and perhaps some foreshadowing of the strength I would call upon to bear many future ordeals in my life, I mention it now because the process of getting a tattoo can be very painful. My letters were simple and small, not much worse than a bikini wax. My Phoenix, on the other hand, is of respectable size and has many colors. It took about four hours in one sitting to complete. My friend came along for company but every time he spoke, I felt the needle in my back like a dagger. Once he left, I focused on my breathing. I aligned it with the sound of the needle's whir, and my brain responded to the pain naturally. Thanks to our body's ability to produce dopamine, I sat there for hours and floated along the sound of my breath on the verge of a deep sleep. My mind ruled my body and

I was able to bear the physical torture being done.

As I made my way to the hospital to see Adam, I felt that way again. Doped up by some miraculous means of my mind, aimed to protect my heart of the new torture it faced. According to Arnon, Beth found out about Adam and I, (though I wasn't sure yet how that happened.) Adam was sick with bipolar disorder, a fact now beyond reasonable doubt. The life I planned with Adam would never come to fruition. Any future life with Adam would be formed as we went along and so far, I was headed to the psych ward at New York Presbyterian.

The music blared as I drove my mom's car, the wind ran through my hair. I ignored the fact all truths had been revealed. In the brief moments I allowed myself to take in the weight of the struggle I faced, I focused on my breath and soon after my rigid limbs grew warm and calm. God bless dopamine.

When I arrived at the hospital, they told me Adam was on the 6th floor. As I rode up in the elevator, I recalled an argument we once had when Adam was still married and living with Beth. I pointed out her legal rights to him if God forbid he were ever hurt or sick in the hospital. I wanted to be the one by his side, not her. The situation dripped with irony.

The doors to the ward were locked. I buzzed for entry. Ana stood at the end of a long hallway, waiting for me outside Adam's room. Part of me expected her to be angry, but she greeted me with a hug. All that mattered was we both loved Adam.

"Brace yourself," warned Ana.

I saw Adam before he saw me. He stood across from his father in some type of small fit. He wore a bright, green, Arabic robe that went to the floor, Jesus style. He wore colorful necklaces and rings. He carried on like a boy having a tantrum, whining, sobbing and frothing at the mouth. Arnon took it like a champ. He behaved like a dad with a young child, not a father with a grown son gone mad. He was calm and patient.

I could tell he had done this before.

Adam suddenly noticed me out of the corner of his eye. He instantly stopped his rant and shot a look of daggers in my direction, before he turned his head completely away. I stopped in my tracks and looked to Arnon for a sign.

"Don't do dat to her," Arnon said to Adam. "Dat's Amanda. She loves you."

Arnon whispered something else I couldn't hear, but Adam reluctantly gave in. He turned and walked towards me with chalky lips and glassy eyes of a stranger. He extended his arms mechanically and stumbled against me. He felt like a skeleton. Seconds later, he shoved me off him and returned to his father, refusing to look in my direction or speak to me.

Arnon came over to me. "He feels shame. Dat's why he behaves dis way."

"He hates me," I said.

"No, no. They give him pills. Some shit to calm him down." Arnon waved his hand at Adam. "Dat's why he's like dis. I need to find out the name of the medicine he was supposed to be taking. Do you know?"

I knew about some pill bottles Adam kept in the refrigerator at his apartment. The only time I ever saw him go in there was to get Hooker's heart medication.

"No, I don't." My lack of answers made me feel helpless. "But I'm gonna go feed his cats after this. I can check when I get there."

"You don't need to feed them," said Arnon. "Beth took care of it."

"Oh." ...*Of course she did.*

"I don't think she'll be doing it again. You'll need to do it tomorrow." He turned to his son, "Adam? Amanda is leaving."

Adam looked at me and turned his back without a word.

"Come back tomorrow," said Arnon. He hugged me and kissed my cheek. Ana did the same.

Before I left, I took a chance my friend and lover might still hear me. "I love you, Adam."

As I drove home it felt like I left another dimension. There seemed no fathomable way any of this was possible. Weren't we just laughing together and loving each other a few days ago? Or was it a few months ago? Or was it...*ever?*

Arnon filled me in on the details of what happened when we spoke earlier that morning. Like Ana said, Adam reached out to Beth for help getting to the emergency room over the pain in his back. Not soon after they arrived, his condition revealed itself.

"His back has bothered him for a while now," I said. "There might be something really wrong."

Arnon spoke in his wise, Middle-Eastern way, "The pain my son feels is in his head."

He was right. Adam was diagnosed with bipolar disorder as a teenager. His current state of mind was due to the result of a manic episode, an extreme surge of physical and mental energy coursing through his veins at rapid speed. My ex-boyfriend Sean suffered from the depressive side of the illness, and before you question my pattern of psychologically disturbed men, keep in mind Adam showed no signs of depression. In fact for the most part, his positivity and optimism inspired me. None of it made any sense to me until I did some Internet research later that evening, nestled safely at my mother's.

Several websites offered the same general definitions and checklists of symptoms. Adam met all of them.

'*Extreme levels of high energy*'. . . . I thought about the way Adam bounced around the apartment the past few weeks. '*Less need for rest or sleep*'. . . . I saw the image of him painting his Mason mural, night after night in the wee hours of the morning. '*Tendency to show poor judgment, such as impulsively deciding to quit a job, tendency to make grand and unattainable plans*'. . . . I remembered how he gave up his clients for an uncertain opportunity that fell through, and tales of his plans to achieve world peace.

The symptoms described rapid talk, heightened sex drive and inflated self-esteem. I recounted how many times the past few weeks I wished for Adam's silence, and how rarely it came. I felt the lonely air that remained each time he made love to me then left me for some other task. I thought of how he said he was better than me, the way he held his hand high in the air when describing himself and low to the ground when describing me.

According to what I read, episodes led to reckless behaviors like spending sprees and drug abuse. Adam's demands for money echoed in my ears. Mania meant rapid changes in mood, huge jumps from joyful to irritable, angry and hostile. I could drown in a pool of Adam's tears shed the past few months, so many he claimed stemmed from joy.

The Internet doled out a bleak enough future I turned to Movies on Demand for inspiration. As though it were alphabetical destiny, I found a film certain to offer encouragement. *A Beautiful Mind*, the true story of a love that successfully conquered mental illness. If Russell Crowe and Jennifer Connolly could do it, so could Adam and I. I loved Adam and I wasn't giving up on us. I would do whatever I could to make sure he didn't either.

CHAPTER 14

❖

I
F I WERE TO BASE A FICTIONAL HERO on myself, her tragic flaw
would be the perpetual hope for a happy ending. After all is said and
done, when I look back, that's how I made most of my mistakes on
my journey with Adam; I walked a broken road paved with good intentions.

The next two weeks blur together somewhat and are extremely
painful to sort out in detail. Adam spent the first six of those days in
the hospital. At our first visit, he was wearing a camouflage tank top
with baggy jeans and a military cap. He had more energy than the night
before but was still struggling at times with words and movement. He
sat me on his bed and showed me several sketches he'd done since I last
saw him. I flipped through pages of altered Adams, but when I saw one
of Beth playing an African drum, with several arms in the air, I froze.

"I told her everything," said Adam.

"You did?"

"Yup," he said, "the night she brought me here. Which reminds me,
she still has my computer."

I sat open-mouthed, stunned. "...What exactly did you tell her?"

"I told her everything about the past two years, how I cheated on her, that you moved in with me. . .everything."

We had spent all that time tiptoeing in secret around Beth's feelings, my heart temporarily sacrificed to protect hers. Yet in one broad stroke, he sliced her heart in half, with no regard for consequence. His tone carried a lack of remorse that confused me—another sign this was not the Adam I knew.

"What did she say?" I asked him.

"She was pissed. Said she already knew it, and she knew she wasn't crazy. She hates me. I better get that computer back."

God help me, I hate to admit it, but I felt a tiny bit of satisfaction. I was finally free, winner by decision, unaware this now put me in a whole new prison. How it had happened made me very uncomfortable. Beth didn't need to hear the details about her husband's affair from a manic mind. I wondered if the truth brought her any relief.

Arnon suddenly entered the room and interrupted us. Adam nervously rose to his feet and asked me to help him in the bathroom. His father encouraged me to go.

"Listen," said Adam, "you can't tell my father I said this to you, okay? Promise you won't tell him." He unzipped his pants and began to pee as he spoke.

"Pay attention to what you're doing," I said.

"Amanda! Listen to me."

I looked up at him.

"You need to get me weed," said Adam. "That is my medicine. I need my medicine."

"Adam, you need to take the medicine the *doctors* give you."

"Don't tell me what I need! I am not *taking* their medicine." He looked around to make sure we were alone and dropped his voice to a whisper. "I'm *cheeking* it."

"You're what?" I asked.

"*Cheeking* it. I stick it in my cheek and they think I took it, but I'm not really taking it."

"Adam, you *have* to take the medicine."

"Don't tell me what I have to do! You're the reason I'm in here, and you better not tell my father anything. All I need is my weed. Nick is gonna bring me some, but it's not enough. You need to bring me some, too. I also need cigarettes and deodorant."

I couldn't help but laugh.

He flushed the toilet. "It's not funny. You need to do what I say." He buttoned his pants, but his naked penis remained exposed through his zipper as he stumbled to leave.

"Your penis is sticking out."

He gazed down at his member hanging flaccidly on the wrong side of his pants and looked up at me longingly. "Could you fix it?"

"Sure. C'mere." He was an overgrown child who couldn't dress himself.

We spent a little bit more time together with Arnon before I left. I planned to stop at the apartment and feed the cats, give Hooker her heart pill, and pay some basic bills to keep things going while Adam was gone. I would come back and see him afterward.

It was my first time back in Brooklyn since the horrible events a few days before, when my life became quicksand. It was supposed to be my home—all of my things were there—but it felt more like the scene of a crime as I approached the front doors. My heart sped up, and my limbs felt like jelly. In an attempt to avoid the neighbors, I hurried quickly upstairs and made it inside without any disturbance.

Once I locked the door behind me, I felt more at ease. I kicked off my shoes and proceeded to move about the rooms as one does when they come home. I tidied up, grabbed a drink from the fridge, made sure cable and electric were paid up for the month. After a quick shower, I would give the cat her medicine and make my way back to the hospital.

The stress of the past few days had my stomach in knots, but as I started to feel at home, I loosened up, and regularity kicked in. I suddenly needed the toilet badly and sat down without closing the bathroom door. There I sat on the toilet in the silence of my thoughts, with my pants around my ankles, when a metallic sound caught my attention. It quickly grew louder and resembled the click of a key in the front door. It had to be the neighbor's door; the only other person with a key was Adam, and I would've heard if he managed to escape.

"Hello?" I called out from the bathroom. No one answered, but the sound was distinctly a key. It mastered the top lock and moved on to the bottom. *"Hello?"* I yelled, waiting for any response.

I heard the door open. Someone was in the apartment, and I was literally caught with my pants down, at any moment about to be found.

"Hello!" I shouted. "Hello, who's there?!" No answer. I heard footsteps inside and a thud through the wall, followed by the clang of keys against the ground. I sat utterly still, completely vulnerable to whoever was standing on the other side of the wall. Seconds later, the door slammed shut. The intruder was gone.

Once the fear faded, I wiped my ass and ran to the living room to see what had happened. Adam's laptop case lay on the couch, his charger thrown haphazardly atop it, and extra house keys rest below on the floor. I heard the building door slam, and it hit me: *Oh, my God. . .Beth!*

I watched through the bedroom window to spot her move up the street. She didn't, but I felt her anger linger in the air around me like puffs of fury trailing her exit.

Had Adam's ex-wife really just walked in on me *taking a shit?* My range of emotions reached a new threshold. I imagined how my voice must've cut through her when she heard me call out. I put myself in her place and felt lucky the situation hadn't turned out worse. Hell hath no fury. . .I doubt *I* could have returned my crazy ex-husband's computer, unharmed, to the home we built together, only to find his mistress living the life I was supposed to, without it ending badly. Then again, I always said Beth was a class act, and in a weird way, she had proved it again.

My mind was elsewhere, fairly freaked out by the entire situation. So much had been happening, and all of it was playing a movie in my head as I showered and got dressed. My hands trembled. Halfway out the door, I realized I had forgotten to give Hooker her medicine.

When I opened the refrigerator door, there were at least four pill bottles on the shelf from which I had seen Adam take Hooker's pills. I didn't know the name of the prescription, but I remembered him giving her half a small, round, white pill. I took a bottle labeled *Clonazepam*. The name meant nothing to me, but when I opened it I saw half a pill that fit the description. I held Hooker in my arms, put the half a pill in her mouth, and waited until she swallowed. I took a last glance at the Macbook adapter on the couch and the keys thrown below it. The image stuck with me the entire trip back to the hospital.

When I told Adam what had happened, he laughed at first, because, let's face it, who wouldn't? Only I could come that close to danger while taking a dump and live to talk about it.

"At least my computer is safe," said Adam. "Did you bring the other stuff?"

I handed him a bag with deodorant and a pack of cigarettes.

"Where's the weed?"

"Adam, I'm not bringing weed into a psych ward. You need to take the meds they're giving you."

His demeanor changed instantly. "*God*, Amanda!" he exclaimed. "The one thing I ask of you, and you can't just do what I ask!"

"Adam, I—"

"No, you don't care. Nick came and brought me weed mixed into a smoothie. That's what a real friend does! He understands. He understands I need my real medicine!" cried Adam.

"I'm sorry, but—"

"But *nothing*. You need to go. Come back tomorrow and bring me what I asked for."

"...You want me to *leave?*" I asked. "I just *got* here! Do you have any clue what I'm going through?"

"It's always about *you. You, you, you.* Poor little piggy."

"Fuck you, Adam." I grabbed my bag and walked out.

He mocked me: "Little piggy's going to cry...."

I had taken the train to the hospital and needed to stop back at the apartment to get my car, which also gave me the chance to use the bathroom before the long trip back. When I entered, I saw Hooker struggling to walk. Something was wrong, *terribly wrong*. She seemed dizzy; every time she stood up, she would fall down again. When she was first diagnosed with heart disease, the vet had said that, over time, her joints would stiffen and she might find it hard to use her legs. *This can't be happening now,* I thought. I couldn't let Hooker die on my watch. With Adam in the hospital. . . . It simply couldn't happen.

I remembered Joni, the neighbor downstairs, had a dog. We met the day I moved in. She was working from home while she and her husband expected their first baby. Despite her friendship with Beth, she had pleasantly offered her help if I ever needed it. Frantic, I ran downstairs and knocked on her door. She gave me the number of a nearby vet, and I quickly called to tell them I was on my way.

As fast as possible, I wove through Brooklyn with Hooker nestled in her carrier next to me. At a point when I thought things couldn't get worse, it felt like a dream. Hooker's sickness had caused a profound stress in Adam, if she died. . . well, I couldn't go there.

The vet saw us fairly quickly. I explained it was my boyfriend's cat, and that he was sick in the hospital. He didn't know we were there. He *couldn't* know we were there. She seemed to understand. A few minutes into the exam, she asked if Hooker was on any meds. I told her about the heart disease and explained I had given her Clonazepam. I'd brought the bottle along just in case.

"You gave this to the cat?" asked the doctor concerned.

"Um—" my palms began to sweat— "yeah."

"How much did you give her?"

"Half a pill."

"This is not medicine for a cat," said the doctor. "This is for a human. What made you give her this pill?"

How was I supposed to explain I was half out of my mind because my psychotic boyfriend's ex-wife had walked in on me while using the toilet? "My boyfriend is in the hospital, and I didn't know the name of the medicine. It looked just like the pill I'd seen him give her before— it was even cut in half the way he does it."

"I need to call a specialist," replied the doctor. "Clonazepam is an anti-anxiety medication for humans. Her symptoms could be the result of the drug or the result of her heart disease. We'll start her on fluids to flush out her system, and hopefully we've caught it in time. Leave her with us, and I'll call you when I have more news."

As I left for my car, it felt like a tornado had ripped through my gut. Before I could check the six missed calls from Adam and two from Ana on my cell, she called again and snapped me from my stupor.

"Hello, Ana?"

"Amanda! Where have you *been*?"

"Something happened to Adam's cat. I don't know what to do. I don't think I should tell him anything until I have more information."

"That's why I'm calling," said Ana. "He already knows."

The world as I knew it slowed to a halt. "What? *How*?"

"Beth told him."

"How does Beth know?" I asked.

"The neighbor told her. They're friends, I guess. She called Beth and told her you showed up panicked over the cat.

Joni and Beth: Of *course*—they were friends. Telling Adam about Hooker was a good way to hit us both at the same time. "How did he react?"

"He's actually better than I expected," said Ana. "He called me looking for you. I think he just wants to know what's going on. You should give him a call."

"I don't know how to tell him this."

"What exactly happened?" asked Ana.

"I gave the cat the wrong medicine. The doctor isn't sure if she's sick because of that or her heart disease." There was a long silence on the other end. "Ana, are you still there?"

"Listen to me," she replied. "Never repeat what you just told me to anyone, ever again. I'm going to forget you ever said it. You make sure the doctor never says it to Adam. He can't know you gave his cat the wrong meds."

"Trust me," I told her, "I'm way ahead of you."

"Good luck," said Ana. "Watch out for that neighbor, she's not your friend."

On autopilot, I drove back towards my mother's house. Adam called every few minutes, but I couldn't face him without more answers. Fortunately I never mentioned the medication to Joni when we spoke, so though I cursed Beth for telling Adam, if Ana and the vet kept their mouths shut, I should be safe. If Adam knew the truth, I seriously thought he might take vengeance on me. In fact, I counted the ways he might take vengeance on me the entire ride home.

The vet finally called as I sat in a parked car down the street from my mom's to have one last cigarette before I recounted it all for my family.

"Ms. Hirsch, it turns out Hooker's condition is a result of her heart disease and not the wrong medication."

I literally felt the weight of manslaughter lift off my shoulders. "I didn't poison her?"

"Well, it didn't help her situation," said the doctor, "but according to the specialist I spoke to, she would've had to take a much larger dose to have a negative effect such as this."

"Oh thank God." I sighed in relief.

"She's still very sick."

Relief came and went. "How sick?" I asked.

"Hooker requires major surgery to save her," she replied. "There's no guarantee and it's quite expensive."

The hits just kept coming. "How expensive?"

"Well, with the treatment so far and the bare minimum costs, we're looking at starting rates around $1,400.00"

"*What?* Are you *kidding* me?" I almost swallowed my tongue.

"As I said, her condition is fairly extensive. I hate to say it but my suggestion is to let her go peacefully."

There it was. A painful truth I had no choice but to face. "I can't make that decision." I didn't notice I started to sob between words.

"Ms. Hirsch," calmed the doctor, "you don't have to make this decision now."

"You don't understand," I cried. "She's not even my cat! I can't tell my boyfriend I killed his cat, I can't! And I don't have $1400 either. My God, what am I gonna do?"

"Please calm down," she said. "We'll continue to give Hooker fluids and keep her comfortable until you have a chance to speak to your boyfriend and make a decision."

"Thank you," I said.

My head rest heavy against the back of my seat. Home was three minutes away, but I couldn't conceive the concept of driving. As if he sensed my torment, Adam called again. While I hated to answer, I couldn't continue without his input and the longer I kept it from him, the worse it would be to come clean.

"Hi Adam."

"I've been trying to reach you all day! What happened to Hooker?"

LOVING ADAM

With a deep breath I told him the status of Hooker's condition. Then I listened as he cried. After a few minutes, he thanked me for taking her to the vet and told me not to bother with the surgery, she was too sick to survive and he wanted her at peace. I told him if we did nothing, she would likely pass away before he got out of the hospital. Through tears and sobs, he asked if I would go back to the vet and say good-bye for him.

"Can you take a picture of her for me?" he asked softly.

"A picture?" It seemed a somewhat morbid concept, but I could remember the urge to snap a photo of both my grandpa and my father as they rest peacefully in their coffins. I hesitated because someone I can't remember told me it was a bad idea. They said my last memories should be of their life, not their death. Yet, a piece of me still wished I'd captured all stages. "Are you sure you want that image in your head, Adam?"

"Do as I ask, please," he answered.

"I'll go tomorrow."

"Are you planning to come to the hospital tomorrow?" he asked.

"I was planning to visit you after the vet, yes."

"Will you stop and see Cleo? She's probably missing Hooker a lot."

"Yes, Adam, I'll spend some time with Cleo too." I felt like a rock cloaked in pain.

"Thank you," he said. "Have a good night."

"Sweet dreams," I whispered, the way we always used to before bed. Adam hung up.

Ready for the last mile home, I wiped the tears from my eyes and turned the ignition. When I walked in, my family sat together watching TV in the living room. They looked so warm and bright compared to the dark world I came from. I sat on the couch clearly drained. They paused the DVR to ask what happened.

"Well first Beth walked in the apartment as I took a shit, then I almost killed Adam's cat."

With that, I became the entertainment. Shock and awe formed across each face as they listened to my antics. It's hard to tell a true story that rivals fiction, without inspiring a dark laugh or two.

"You didn't kill the cat," said my sister. "The vet said it was her heart."

My mother chimed in, "That won't matter to him. You better hope he never finds out about it, or bye-bye Oliver."

"Mommy!" shouted my sister, "Don't say that, you'll scare her."

"We don't know what this man is capable of," said my mother.

"Oh God," I said, "what if she's right? What if he comes after Oliver?"

"The two of you need to stop," said Debbie. "Just explain to the vet Adam's condition and why he can't know about the pills. I'm sure she doesn't want retaliation on her hands."

Again, Debbie made sense of a completely nonsensical situation. I sunk back deep against the cushions and sighed heavily.

"Pardon my language," I said out of respect for my twelve year-old niece in the room, "but how the *fuck* did I get here?"

"I honestly have no idea," said Debbie as she resumed her paused program, "but don't worry, you'll get through it."

CHAPTER 15

❖

O N THE WAY TO BROOKLYN the next day, I picked up a disposable camera to honor Adam's wish for a picture of Hooker before she passed. Despite the bizarre circumstances that surrounded me, I still imagined all of it was temporary. Arnon said if Adam took his medicine, he would get better. He was in the hospital under doctor supervision. By default that meant he had to improve, right?

Wrong. When I got to his room, Adam asked if I saw the cat and I replied yes, I would drop off the film to be developed on my way home.

"Did you bring me what I asked for, Amanda?"

"I told you Adam, I'm not bringing weed in here. You need to listen to the doctors."

He smiled calmly. "It doesn't matter, I'm getting out of here anyway. I have other people here willing to help me."

"Are they in the room with us now?" I asked, half in jest.

"No—" Adam paused briefly to scan the room. "One of the orderlies is a Mason," he winked.

"How lucky for you," I said. How unlucky for the rest of us, I thought.

"My brothers are everywhere looking out for me," beamed Adam. "This one saw the pin in my wallet when I checked in. One of the security guards is a Mason too. Both of them are looking out for me."

I hoped the story was either a delusion or some type of new hospital treatment for his disorder, but Adam believed it enough to make me worry. It sounded more like a scene straight from a movie: enablers lodged within the asylum to breed crazy rather than cure it.

"Amanda, I was thinking. . . . I know things didn't work out as we planned, but I'd like us to be friends. I would like if you move near me so we can still hang out."

His words hit hard. He sounded very sane whenever he talked about the end of our relationship. I had to remind myself he was sick.

"Actually," I answered, "I was thinking about moving to Queens."

"Oh, c'mon," he laughed in my face. "You know if you move to Queens I'll never come see you. It's so far."

"Wow." I thought about all I had done for Adam the past few days, the past few years. The strong, confident Mandy my mother had raised peeked out from the cloud of doom that faced me and reminded me I deserved more. "Do you have any idea how many miles I traveled for you since all this happened?" I asked. "I paid your bills, took care of your cat. I gave up my apartment and had your wife walk in on me while indisposed!"

"Look," he said calmly and with a straight face, "I appreciate you paying the bills, but let's face it: You're the reason I'm in here."

"*I'm* the reason?" I could feel my cheeks turning red. Soon steam would be coming out of my ears.

"You beat me," answered Adam. "You wouldn't give me my medicine."

My jaw hung open a moment before I spoke. "I'm gonna get going."

"You know it's true," he went on. "You behave like a wild banshee."

"That's it!" I said. "I'm done."

"There you go again," he taunted.

"Adam, *you* broke up with *me*. You kicked me out of the *house*. You claim I'm a wild banshee who beats you. You have no reason to want to stay in touch with me. Throw away my things and have a good life."

He called me piggy as I stormed out down the hall. Before I reached the exit, I turned towards a group of nurses huddled behind protective glass. "That man is crazy and playing all of you. If you let him out and something bad happens, it's on you."

One nurse became particularly combative. "Don't threaten me!"

"I'm not threatening you, I'm warning you he's unstable. He's not taking his meds."

She pointed at me when she said, "What that boy does is *not* my responsibility."

With such an attitude, I wondered how often that woman released patients who weren't ready to go and whether the guilt of that fact ate away at her. But it didn't seem wise to argue with a nurse in a psychiatric ward. Besides, I didn't care. I was done with all of it, ready to reclaim some level of normalcy.

Back at Adam's apartment, I took as much of my stuff as I could fit into the car, ready to part with anything I left behind. My refusal to quit on love I had once felt morphed into an acceptance of what I couldn't control. I gave Cleopatra one last hug and apologized for the new world I had left her in.

The noise in my head drowned out the radio on the way home; I was a single woman over thirty with no place to live, forced to start over because the man she once loved had switched personalities. It all seemed so surreal, but Adam was out of my life, and time marches on.

Sadly, this experience would never be that easy. My feelings of closure lasted about twenty-four hours. That's how long it took before Adam resurfaced in my world.

A flurry of people sent me emails and text messages that Adam had been released. The neighbor who'd sold me out to Beth when the cat got sick sent me updates on Adam's behavior, each one more bizarre than the next. She complained he played loud rap music all the time and showed up at their apartment several times a day looking for company. Adam had all this energy, and not enough places to put it. She and her husband contemplated moving.

Adam's plot against taking his meds proved a success, and his mania remained. The bugger about mental illness is that one must pose a physical threat to themselves or society before they can be forced to get treatment. If neither of those are the case, they can behave however they want, often leading to self-destruction and the alienation of external relationships.

Adam's harassment eventually returned with demands I pay him rent money minus bills I had covered while he was in the hospital.

Adam also claimed I owed him a new Macbook charger. The day Beth returned the computer as I was relieving myself, she had tossed the charger on top of the laptop case rather than inside it. Cleopatra had a habit of chewing through any wire she could find, and destroyed it. Adam said I should have known what Cleo would do, and since I left the charger out, I was responsible for what had happened and had to buy him a new one. He added it to my tab.

Through a grapevine of mutual friends and former co-workers, I also got word Beth was officially done with Adam, and that Naz, his former buddy from the gym, had filled the void. When Naz had had enough, Adam moved on to an old friend from high school named Dale.

A competitive Muay Thai fighter, Dale had a crass demeanor that instantly turned me off. Every other phrase he spoke contained profanity. Dale had no filter. But he had been there for Adam during one of his previous episodes, which made Adam loyal to him and me tolerant. My concern was that, with Dale, Adam had the brawn to back up his mouth. That could only lead to trouble.

Adam's father kept telling me it was okay to move back to the apartment, and that Adam needed me. Then I'd get an update from the neighbor that Adam jumped out his window and climbed down the rear of the house to avoid a visit from Arnon, convinced he was coming with the authorities.

My family banned me from going back. Truth was none of us had been in such a situation before and our best hope was to ignore it in the hope that, eventually, Adam would tire and go away. It might have worked, if not for the fact that bipolars in a hyper-manic state rarely tire.

At 1:39 a.m. on July 24, Adam left me the following message:

> *Hey hon, it's me. I just wanna let you know that. . .I'm goin' through a lotta stuff now, and I'm just gonna need your help. So when I call you, just try to call me back, and just check up on me as well, ya know, periodically. I am fighting a battle and we are gonna get these properties. . .and I just wanna let you know. . .just call me and make me feel comfortable, that's all I need. . .and all I want. And I love you. Talk to you soon. . .bye.*

He knew what was happening to him. It reminded me of our talk in the shower months before when he tried, in his own warped way, to warn me of his condition. Between the battles for real estate properties at war in his mind, he was asking for help and support, reaching out in peace. The man I loved remained inside him, but it was the last time I heard his echo.

Later that day (as I have already said in the opening pages of this story), well after the sun had risen and parted the noon sky, Adam called me to tell me his dead cat was in his freezer. He demanded I give him a ride to pick up new kittens somewhere in Nassau County, and I demanded he see the only therapist I knew he trusted. He threatened to blow up my house. I threatened to call the police. Until then, I hadn't allowed that thought to occur to me. He called back shortly thereafter, at 3:32 p.m., and left another message.

> Hey Amanda, it's me. Sorry about that, I was in pain. Just about to go to the police station. I got an email about the two kittens, I'm actually gonna get the male Blue-point and also the female as well. I'm gonna get both of them. I'm gonna ask a friend of mine if I could use the car and get it tomorrow, or if you're able to let me use it, or drive it or. . . um . . .I'll ask my Dad or Pilar to put it on their credit card, because I don't have enough on the card, but I'll be able to pay the cash, as long as I have the $150 you promised me. And I appreciate everything, and I'm sorry again. Just realize I'm in pain, okay? I love you.

I ignored him. Bomb threats and police reports meant things were escalating, and I needed some space to process it. He left another message at 1:04 the next afternoon, his tone less apologetic and more entitled, sternly asking for transportation to pick up the kittens. I ignored him again but admit I considered helping him. I knew he was agonizing over the loss of Hooker, and maybe these kittens would give him something to come back to earth for. That's why I answered when he called back a few minutes later. This time his voice cold as he ordered me to help him. He threatened to call the cops if I didn't give him his money. Again I told him I wouldn't give him anything until I knew he'd seen a professional, and I hung up the phone. Refusing to let him bully me, I refused to answer his next call.

At 1:20, he left me this message:

> Hello, it's me. I just want to inform you officers from the Seventy-second Precinct will be coming to take information from you, and that's it! And I will be suing you, and I will be having your check garnished, and you won't have money 'cause your check will be garnished. What you did, what you said, how

you beat me. . . . In my own home! And we have a lotta people that know about how you beat me. Now the [inaudible] is coming to get you, woman! Alright? For beating me! And then your fuckin' tellin' me your not gonna give me the money you owe me, after you beat me, that you said that you had to? Alright. You'll find my fury.

As I hung up, a heavy sigh parted my lips. In a little over a day Adam had gone from asking for help and support, to threats of suffering and jail if he didn't get it. In a sixteen-minute span, two messages and a conversation only began to illustrate how bad things could get.

CHAPTER 16

❖

O N Friday, July 25, at 2:00 P.M., Adam raised the stakes a notch. I hadn't thought it would be possible. But it was. He did it by treating me to another rambling voicemail:

Hello, this is Adam. I just wanted to let you know that, tomorrow, I'd like to come to the observation deck. And I would like a comp pass, I want you to arrange it, and I wanna take pictures from the deck and draw. Alright? I'm at the Seventy-second Precinct, and I'm getting a report filed against you. I will not take you to court maybe. . . maybe. . .I won't take you to court if you could arrange for me, and one of my brother Masons, to come to the observation deck, and realize, even if you try to stop us, then you will be thrown in jail immediately. And your job will be lost, and you will never work in New York City again. Okay? I have already arranged that, if you do go against my wishes, everyone knows you beat me. I have many witnesses. They're hearing everything. Even my neighbors heard everything. So do you get me? Realize August 1st, that you owe me. . .actually, no! The six hundred dollars you owe me, you can deduct whatever you paid for my bills, but you're gonna pay me what you owe me of that half month's rent. Okay? 'Cause I'm not letting you freeload, I'm gonna take you to court as well, if you don't give me and deduct everything you give me in terms of my bills and minimal hundred dollars you're gonna have to give me. And tomorrow, I want to go to the observation deck, for free. You will arrange that or you go to jail. You tell your mom that her daughter will be in jail, and there will be no bail. There will be no bail. I'll make sure that your ass is fucked really good, in jail. And I don't mean that in terms of just them, ya know, allowing what you did to me. Alright? You could record this, you could show this conversation to anybody, but you beat me. Alright? You beat me, and you made me go to the hospital, alright? You made me fear for my life, and you're gonna go to jail if you don't do what I ask. And that's not blackmail, I'm asking for you to give me what you owe me, but I'm also filing a report, and I'm most likely gonna have charges anyways pressed against you because you deserve it. Goodbye.

For the first time I felt scared. His strange desire to visit my work, and his conviction about sending me to jail, made me wonder how far all this could go. His specific comments about my mother and my future prison rape crossed new, *violent* lines. Never mind the fact all this was coming from a man I knew to be a pacifist.

I thought more and more about contacting the police, but Adam kept saying he had filed a report against me. With my luck, a complaint from me could somehow lead to my arrest. Instead I called Arnon. He seemed to be able to handle Adam to whatever extent anyone could.

"I will take care of it," he said in a voice astute enough to fool me.

Things quieted down for a couple of days. The gaps between Adam's calls widened. On the morning of July 27, he left a message in a soft voice, claiming everything was great. As sweetly as he could, he again asked for a computer charger and a ticket to the observation deck. I handled it the best way I knew how. I did nothing.

I couldn't allow Adam to visit my place of business. My company had permitted me to use my vacation time to deal with all this, and I needed it resolved before I went back to work. As long as it was far from any resolution, I had to keep a safe distance between my professional and personal lives. Adam used his threats to hit me in a sacred spot he knew I cared about. A threat to my livelihood made me more amenable to his demands. Still, I did nothing, as I often do when faced with a situation I don't have a clear solution for. I prefer to let the clock tick on in the hope events unfold that help sway me.

It was almost midnight, and Adam's birthday crept upon me. All day I thought of this moment approaching. Between hourly updates to my family on the status of his silence, I fantasized about the birthday we could've shared together. I agonized over the turn of the tide away from us. It had been meant to be our first birthday together as a happy couple. The year before, he had said we'd have "many more birthdays together." The man plans, and God laughs.

By 12:01 a.m., I caved. At the top of my basement stairs, I dialed Adam's phone. When I got his voicemail, I left a message, for my sake more than his. It started with happy birthday and acknowledged the irony of his comment the previous year. At the end I said I loved him and always would.

Seconds later, he returned the call. Out of weakness, I answered.

"Hi, Amanda!" His voice was full of excitement.

"Hi, Adam. Happy birthday."

"Thanks. Oh, it's already such a great birthday!"

That hurt a little. "Is it?"

"Oh yeah, you don't know the things I've seen! Last night I went to Prospect Park, and I lay in the grass on my back and just stared up at the stars. You won't believe what happened." He started to choke up with emotion.

"What happened?" I asked.

"I saw things, Amanda. *They came to me.*"

"Who came to you?"

"*Them.* The creatures that exist that no one sees. But I saw them!

The last time I got sick, I saw them! And they came to me again, last night, right there in the park!"

"You're saying invisible creatures hung out with you last night in Prospect Park?"

"Yes, and Amanda, they'll let you see them. Because you're beautiful and special, and because I told them you're my queen."

As good as it felt to hear him say something remotely nice about me, I winced slightly at the volume of his delusions. I couldn't bask in compliments surrounded by insanity. It didn't seem fair to selectively choose Adam's truths. He did that just fine on his own. Still, he sounded happy. He cried tears of joy as he spoke about the night sky full of stars and his imaginary heroes who revealed their secrets of the Universe. The creatures he referred to undoubtedly meant aliens from another planet. Adam swore by their existence. Aside from the Sitchen books, I had seen shelves of literature on the topic when I moved in. I shared his belief in extraterrestrials, but mine stemmed from an open mind. His apparently stemmed from an experience he had had during a previous episode that made his conviction all the more powerful.

I listened to his detailed description of their appearance and his warnings of how I would now see them since he had spoken to me. Yet the more I listened, the more it was my own thoughts I heard, wondering again how the fuck I'd gotten there.

"Oh, by the way," he said. "I'm joining the army."

". . .You're what?" I must have skipped a beat somewhere.

"I'm joining the army. The Iranian army! *Fuck the American army.*"

I can't recall his reasoning, mainly because I got stuck wondering how soon it would be before Homeland Security showed up on my doorstep. The pacifist had suddenly turned rebel and traitor in one breath.

"Adam, please don't say these things."

"It's the truth! I have dual citizenship. I have an Iranian passport!

They will gladly take me. I'm leaving in a week, and you won't see me again for a very long time."

I sighed. "Well. . . . If that's what you want."

"It's gonna be great!" he said.

"Listen, Adam, I really just called to wish you a happy birthday and let you know I was thinking of you."

"Thank you, Amanda. I better get going. I have a lot to get ready. I love you."

It never failed to surprise me how Adam could crush me entirely and so easily cap it off with *I love you.* When I hung up the phone, I thought about everything he had said, and though it made me sad, a piece of me felt relieved at the thought of him leaving the country, never to be seen or heard by me again. For the first time, I didn't mind the thought of him being crazy, if it meant I'd finally be left alone, able to move on.

On his actual birthday, I lingered in my front yard as a few neighbors and their children stopped by my family's home for a little summer socializing. The adults relaxed in lawn chairs on the driveway, while the older kids played basketball around us. My sister sipped on a Mike's Hard Lemonade, and my mother laughed along with the small talk and banter that flew between us. People wore shorts and flip-flops. The toddlers ran around the grass. The beauty of the moment struck me in a way I felt no one else there could equally appreciate. This was their everyday life, part of their routine. I had always been a young, single girl who could do whatever she wanted, too cool for "PTA" stuff. Yet there I was, for the first time in my life, envious of such simple pleasures as family, stability, security, and. . .oh yeah, *sanity.*

My phone rang. It was Dory calling from the old gym I used to work at, the one where Adam and I began.

"Hi, Dory!" I answered happily.

"Amanda!" she gasped. "Have you heard from Adam?"

My mood darkened. "No, not since last night. I wished him a happy birthday."

"Well, he just came to Thirteenth Street, saying all sorts of horrible things about you," said Dory.

I froze in my tracks. My stomach churned. She went on despite my silence. "He claimed you pulled a knife on him and you beat him! He even started a fight with Kai. Who starts a fight with Kai?"

It was tough to imagine anyone intentionally starting an argument with Kai. He was a gay aerobics instructor with a thick Japanese accent. His favorite words were *kiss-kiss* and *honey*. More importantly, Kai was Adam's friend. They'd worked together when Adam was at the gym. Kai had given him a *Kama Sutra* book as a wedding gift when he married Beth. He used to cat-sit for them when they went on vacation, but Kai and I were also very close. When Kai heard of the divorce and how Adam and I had fallen in love, he'd supported both of us without question or criticism.

"Any chance you're joking?" I asked.

"No." Dory barely paused to take a breath. "He came in super-agitated and started going off on you at the front desk."

"At *me*? Were there any members around?"

"At first it was just a few of us. Kai had just finished with a client. He tried to calm Adam down when he started screaming you threatened him with a knife."

"Good God." I felt faint.

"Then he called Kai a faggot and told him to shut his mouth before he smacked him like a little bitch. That's when Paul got involved."

Paul was the new personal training manager and a former Golden Gloves fighter—a recipe for potential disaster. "Did he hit Adam?" Half of me wanted to hear that Paul had knocked the psychotic chip off Adam's block.

"No," said Dory. "Paul could see Adam was off his rocker. He just wanted to stop the scene in the lobby. I thought he might do something when Adam called him *a little man*, but afterwards he said it wasn't worth going to jail for. His punch is registered."

"Shit," I whispered.

"Anyway, Adam mentioned something about blowing up Twenty-third Street, so our CEO canceled his membership and filed a report with the police. He made me 'n Paul go to the precinct to give a statement."

"How *Law & Order*," I teased. "You must've loved it."

"My armpits wouldn't stop sweating!" cried Dory. "I told Paul I was afraid I would be arrested because I had pills on me. Sure, I had a prescription, but I was convinced they were gonna lock me up. Gotta love my Jewish guilt."

Somehow I managed to laugh. "Does everyone now think I pulled a knife on Adam?"

"I think we're all more *worried* about you than anything else," said Dory. The CEO asked for your cell number. He said he wanted to make sure you were okay."

Lovely. My former hard-ass boss now knew about my affair with Adam and, worse, what an oblivious fool I'd been. It didn't matter to me that I no longer worked there; Adam had set out to destroy my reputation in a place he knew mattered deeply to both of us. There was no rational reason for him to involve the gym. His path to destruction included all the stops that had once meant anything in his life, the pain and loss of friendships collateral damage.

When I hung up with Dory, I told my family the news. They said things had gone too far and demanded I call the police. First I called and left a message for my cousin, a former A.D.A. turned criminal defender. Then my sister suggested we reach out to a neighbor, a recently retired detective from a Harlem precinct.

He advised me to file an official report with his precinct. He felt

Adam was escalating, and that my inability to imagine him becoming violent no longer meant that he wouldn't. The Adam I had known was gone, and no one else could say with certainty what had taken his place. My neighbor knew better than any of us what someone in Adam's mindset was capable of. I told him that Adam said he would have me arrested, and that I was afraid to talk to the police. He told me not to worry and gave me the name of a female cop in the Domestic Violence Division who would help me.

Before I left for Harlem, I called Arnon to tell him what had happened. He muttered something under his breath in a foreign language. "Don't worry, it will be okay," he tried to assure me.

"How are you holding up?" I asked him.

"I'm not feeling so good," he answered. "I'm not sure why or what's wrong. I just don't feel well."

"You don't know why?" I asked in shock. "With the level of stress you're under, I don't know how you're doing it!"

Arnon was probably in his mid-fifties to low sixties, and looked like he weighed a hundred pounds soaking wet. Factor in two packs of Marlborough Reds a day with the stress of Adam, and I anticipated an imminent collapse.

"You think that's what it is?" he asked. "*Stress?*"

For a man who so often sounded wise, his denial astounded me. "Yes, Arnon. You need to take care of yourself, too."

Again I heard foreign words I don't think I was meant to hear. "Well don't worry," he said. "I will take care of this. I love you. Bye."

"Love you too, bye."

"Who was that?" asked my sister as she and my mother entered the room.

"Arnon," I said.

"You tell him you love him?"

"He tells me he loves me. I'm not gonna leave him hanging."

My mother stopped the faucet. ". . .Adam's father tells you he loves you?"

"Yeah."

"You don't think that's strange?"

"I think he's as lost by everything going on as we are. I don't know why he says it, or even if it's true, but I guess it makes us feel better. Like we're the only two people left who love Adam. Maybe he thinks it makes us family."

"That's kinda sweet," said my mother.

"Yeah. . . . Well, I'm off to the Harlem Domestic Violence Division to see about filing charges against the love of my life. Let's hope I don't end up arrested in the process." Sweet had no place in my world.

"Fingers crossed!" said my sister.

The hour drive to the city felt longer than usual, as if the burden I bore weighed down my wheels the way it crushed my shoulders. As had so often been the case lately, I had no idea what to expect.

At the desk I asked for Officer Mendez. The sergeant told me to take a seat while I waited. Eventually a female officer approached with an inmate in tow. She handed him off to another officer and turned to face me. "You must be Amanda," she said with a smile.

"Yes," I answered nervously. She led me down the hall into a small office where her male partner was sitting. Both of them clearly knew some detail about me before I got there.

"Miss Hirsch," began the male officer, "my name is Officer Ramirez. On the phone earlier, you told Officer Mendez that your ex claims to have a complaint filed against you. Is that right?"

"Yes. That's what he says."

"We checked our system, and we're showing no record of a complaint against you in any of the five boroughs."

Relief spread through my body. "Thank God."

Over the course of the next hour, I relayed to both officers what had happened over the past few weeks. None of it fazed them. They had heard it before, probably more than once. Both conveyed a look that told me they knew how my story ended.

"Miss Hirsch," said Mendez. "I strongly suggest filing a complaint of harassment and allow us to pursue an order of protection against Mr. Haddad."

It wasn't what I wanted to hear. "An order of protection? Do you think he's violent? He's never been violent before."

Officer Mendez showed slight remorse in her eyes. She didn't have the heart to break mine. She glanced across the room to Ramirez, prompting his lead.

"The thing is, Amanda," said Ramirez, ". . .no one ever really knows what someone in Adam's condition is capable of. He's proven he's stuck on you, and it's unlikely he'll let go on his own. Now, I can't say for certain what he'll do, but I've seen too many women sit right where you are, beaten both physically and emotionally because they refused to see the truth when it stared 'em in the face. Are you willing to risk it?" He struggled with compassion. No wonder Mendez had passed the bad news buck.

The air around me felt thick with intensity. The complaint felt more like an obligation than a choice. "What will happen if I do this?"

"We'll issue a warrant for his arrest. Then we'll pick him up," said Ramirez. "He'll spend the night in jail, and he'll be ordered to stay away from you or he goes to prison."

Tears came to my eyes at the word *jail*. The image of the man I love in a cage made me burst into tears.

Mendez handed me a Kleenex on cue. "I know this isn't easy," she said, trying to comfort me. "But it will keep you safe."

I'd like to say I quickly weighed all potential outcomes of the situation before I made a decision, but I didn't. Instead, I thought of Adam holding me close in the shower, vulnerable to inner demons he couldn't quite share. He'd told me that, no matter what happened to him or whatever he said, he would never hurt me. He said it as if he knew I might be forced to consider the choice I was facing someday. Someday was now.

"I'm sorry. I can't do this." I blew my nose and gathered my things. Mendez tried to stop me. Ramirez looked disappointed. "I can't be responsible for sending him to jail. He's sick! I just can't."

"Take my card," said Mendez. "Call me anytime, especially if it gets any worse."

I took the card and forced a smile. "Thank you."

I didn't bother to look at Ramirez. In fact, at that moment I *hated* Ramirez; his love was tough. I was inclined instead to learn the hard way.

CHAPTER 17

❖

WHEN I GOT BACK TO MY CAR, the tears fell. The pressure crushed me, and I longed for anyone to tell me it would be okay. I sat alone in the police precinct parking lot a hysterical mess. If I didn't pull it together, it would draw suspicion. The last thing I needed was a man in blue at my window.

As I pulled into the garage at home, I smelled my mother's cooking through the door. God bless her, she knew her rice and beans always soothed me. Maybe it was meant to celebrate Adam behind bars, but when I told them all I couldn't go through with it, my mom admitted some relief. She still worried Adam might retaliate against me if I put him in jail. First and foremost, she cared about my safety. I was struggling to protect us all, including Adam.

Homemade goodness does wonders to numb the pain. After stuffing my belly with Mom's love, I sank onto one of the living room couches and drooled over Gilles Marini on *Dancing with the Stars*. None of us said a word about Adam. I actually managed to forget the worst of the day.

Just before bed, I plugged my phone in to charge it and noticed a new message. My heart beat slightly faster, and my throat felt dry as I checked it.

The message had been sent at 10:45 p.m. on Monday, July 28. Adam's tone sounded friendly. His words, not so much.

Well, hello there, umm. . . . Yeah I just talked to my dad. He found out about that little gym incident. . . . Which I'm not done burning that place down. . .metaphorically. And you got in my way and called up Daddy. Realize now that I'm gonna have an APB for your arrest, so if you set foot in any of the five boroughs, I will make sure you are A-rrested.

'Cause you are a crazy, psycho-bitch. And ah. . . realize Thursday, you have my charger and a hundred dollars, or they'll just show up at your mom's door and everyone will know and. . . . That's the thing, ya know? I was there charging my phone, at the gym. And then Kai got all snotty. . .all "I'm taking Amanda's side, which is the right side," which obviously didn't include any sick, fucking violence. But realize. . .I won already. And you lost. So. . . just do what I say. Realize you won't go to jail, if you do what I say. Okay? . . . Bye.

Officer Ramirez had said there were no complaints on record against me in his computer system. It eased the threat of an APB or any jail time Adam tried to impose. My freedom was a warm blanket, and I managed to drift off to sleep without the risk of prison rape to keep me awake.

The next day I went to find a new apartment. After the past two weeks in Crazytown, Brooklyn wasn't an option. Queens was a viable alternative. Astoria was known as a young, hip area for those that couldn't afford Manhattan, like Williamsburg or Hoboken. A few of my co-workers lived there and had only nice things to say. At first, I tried some doorman buildings that my salary could cover, but my credit history limited my options. I finally found an adorable, fourth floor walk-up in a small building through Craigslist.

The building had a live-in super (I'll refer to him as "Schneider") who showed me the place. The door opened into a nice living room, with a kitchen to the right and a good-sized bedroom to the left. It was the biggest apartment in my single- living experience, and, unexpectedly, Queens felt like a step in the right direction. Schneider had done some renovations and offered to let me pick the colors for the final paint job. I chose a powder blue for the bedroom, sage for the main room, and eggshell for the kitchen. Then I drove straight to the landlord to sign the lease, effective August 1. I could move in before I went back to work and get used to a new routine.

I recently did some research on how many decisions the average person makes each day and found sources suggesting anywhere from 70 to 35,000. Our brains are exposed to more information in one second than we can comprehend. Subconsciously, our brain helps eliminate irrelevant data before it materializes so we don't become overwhelmed. It would be great if we could subliminally extinguish bad choices before we had the chance to make them, but influential underlying factors that often start at birth shape us along the way.

Did I fully consider moving to Queens? Did I really test the commute or the walk from my door to the train? Did I check out the neighborhood before I put down first, last, and security? No. Adam had infected my decision-making process from the moment he first kissed me, like a contagion. At the time, moving to Queens was about getting back to normal, and I couldn't do that in my mother's house. Not only was it an inconvenience, it kept all of them exposed to the insanity I had placed us all in. I needed to deal with my mess on my own, and rational thought played little part in the process. When I came home and told my family I was moving, of course they asked me all the questions I hadn't asked myself, but, although I had few answers, they didn't stop me either. I think we were all ready for an end to the madness that had engulfed me.

It turned out Arnon and Pilar lived in Maspeth. He promised to have me over for dinner when I told him my plans to move. Whether he meant the invite or not didn't matter to me; I planned to cut the Adam cord ASAP. Arnon spoke with Adam and arranged for me to pick up my things, so I could move to my new home. Whatever transpired between them led Adam to promise us a smooth transition.

"I want his father to be there," said my mother.

"I think he will be." I had no idea but hoped so.

The following morning, Arnon called me shortly after I left my house for the journey to Brooklyn.

"Do me a favor," he said. "Just bring Adam whatever he is asking for—the charger, the money for rent, whatever."

"I have all of that. You're gonna be there, right, Arnon?"

"Could you also get him a birthday gift?" he added.

"A *what?*" I asked.

"A birthday gift. He's lonely. It will make him happy. We need to keep him calm and happy. When you're there, just be nice to him and do your best not to let his comments get to you."

"But you're gonna be there, right?" I asked again.

"Yes, yes. I'll be there. Just get him a present. Bye-bye."

I took the back-road shortcut to the highway; there wasn't a store in sight except for a seasonal farmer's market a few feet ahead. Frantically, I scoured the tables for something I could pass as a gift. I grabbed an Azalea plant and a jar of homemade honey, and quickly got back on the road.

Arnon had parked his truck out front of Adam's apartment. I slowly eased up behind him, glad he had kept his word. They approached me together as I gathered up a ransom that included one Macbook charger, an Azalea plant, a jar of honey, and a hundred-dollar bill.

"Hello, Amanda," said Arnon. He glanced at Adam.

"Hello, Amanda," said Adam serenely. "Thank you for the gifts, and don't worry, you don't need my father here. I'm not going to do anything to bother you."

"Here." I gave him the items and smiled.

"Thank you." He appeared sincerely grateful.

"Well," said Arnon, "I have to go."

"*What?*" I asked. "You were supposed to stay here."

"Don't worry Amanda, I'm fine," said Adam. "You'll be fine."

I didn't feel a hundred percent comfortable, but I figured it was best to follow Arnon's advice and keep things copacetic. The goal was to make this quick and easy.

Adam turned to go inside while I cautiously concealed my trepidation.

"Thank you so much for the plant," he said as we walked up the stairs. "You know, flowers remind me of my grandmother. She loved them. When I did the painting of her to win the award, I crushed up flowers from her garden and put them in the painting."

We stopped just outside the door. He turned to face me with tears in his eyes. "This plant makes me feel like she's with me." He smiled with emotion.

"I'm glad, Adam."

"Oh, and the honey! Wait till you see this." He unlocked the door quickly and ran into the kitchen.

When I walked in, I couldn't believe it was the same apartment. It was a total mess. In the bedroom, I saw the mattress I had brought with me when I moved in. The sheets were scattered across the memory foam. On top of the bed, two tiny Siamese kittens were dancing around a puddle of cat piss. Adam came flying in from the kitchen with another jar of honey in his hand.

"Look!" he said, excited. "When the breeders came to bring me my new kittens, they gave me this. They live on a farm and make their own honey."

"Wow, cool." I looked at the kittens.

"That's Zeus and Pandora," said Adam like a proud papa.

"They're adorable," I replied.

I scanned the apartment, once kept in perfect order, and struggled to recognize it amid the muck. It looked like someone had burgled the place but not taken anything. Furniture was placed at odd angles, and the Persian rugs were half rolled up.

"I'm packing," said Adam. "I'm gonna be leaving here soon, too."

In my peripheral vision, I spotted a jar of white powder on an end table. It looked like the powder my grandmother used to wear, the kind that comes in an oyster-shaped box with a fluff puff for your nose. I decided not to ask.

"Well," I said, "I need to start taking my things down."

"Wait, I want to show you something." Adam turned to his dresser and pulled out a leather bag about the size of a shaving kit. He handed it to me.

Inside, I saw a pipe and a tube. He handed me a bag full of crack paraphernalia. I wasn't very familiar with the items, but it felt instinctively wrong to be holding any of them in my hands. Any other day I might've dropped the bag and run, or screamed profanities. It's difficult to predict what I might otherwise have done, though, because I had never been in that situation, nor had I ever thought I would be. I'd actually tried to avoid crack-heads my entire life, yet the man I loved had just handed me a bag full of tools they would sell their soul for. Arnon's advice rang in my ears, and I chose to keep the peace. I closed the bag and gave it back to Adam. "I really don't feel comfortable seeing this."

"It's not mine," said Adam, "it's Nick's."

Sure it was. "Even so," I told him. "I'd rather not see it."

"I'm taking them down, Amanda! For what they did to Nick." Adam took the bag and returned it to a dresser drawer. "They got him hooked on this shit, and I'm gonna make them pay."

"Who did, Adam?"

"The drug dealers!" His expression was more excited than angry.

"You think I'm gonna let them fuck with my best friend? Oh, no. I'm taking them down. I'm putting them in jail where they belong."

"Okay, Adam." What else could I say? Weighing his truth was a daunting task. Everything he said contained elements of fact and fiction. His history mixed with his reality. I made my way to the storage closet to start moving boxes.

I'm not sure why, but a piece of me thought Adam would help me as I moved. He was strong, with tons of energy to spare. He could've cut my burden in half with little effort. Instead, he did the opposite. He let the two kittens run free in the apartment and never bothered to clear the obstacle course that had transformed the floors. I was forced to step over piles of clothing and dodge random book piles as I carried my belongings. Each time I cleared the exit, I welcomed the two flights down to the ground floor. Every now and then he would distract me or physically get in my way, and I had no choice but to humor him.

At one point he decided to show me some pictures on his camera, I can't exactly remember why. As he scrolled, I noticed a recent picture of Naz and some girl sitting in our living room that made me hiss inside.

"Who's she?" I asked.

He stopped the slide show and took the camera away. He didn't need it anymore; he'd found the button he had set out to press.

"That's a girl Naz brought over so I could draw her."

Lo and behold, the knife could go deeper. "You *drew* her? Was she naked?" My hiss dissipated, but my back arched and my hair stood on end.

"Oh, please, Amanda. It was just a drawing. Besides, we're not together anymore, so you can't say anything."

I felt like an elevator with a toddler inside who pressed every button from basement to penthouse, but somehow I kept it together.

"You're right, Adam. You can do whatever you want."

He took that statement literally. He put on loud music, cut me off as I stepped over debris. He charged at me slowly when he spoke, getting closer and closer to the point where I'd take a step back, then he'd stop an inch before my face. He enjoyed seeing me on the brink of fear or rage, and it took everything I had not to sway in either direction.

As I reached the last box, I could tell Adam sensed the end approaching. I made one last turn through each room to make sure I had gotten all the little things. Lord knows I didn't want to have to come back there, ever again. When I left the bedroom, Adam was standing before me in a pale green Egyptian robe that glowed against his tan skin, and he had a turban on his head that framed his face perfectly; his dark eyes and long, thick eyelashes looked exotic. His beauty struck me for a moment. I pitied the future strangers who would be fooled by the depth of his intelligence and his dimples.

"Before you go," said Adam, "I wanna show you something."

That phrase began to send chills down my spine, but I was almost home free. I couldn't risk upsetting the applecart.

"Okay, but I gotta be quick. I still have to unload all this stuff at my new place."

Adam went into a closet and pulled out a Samurai sword, like the ones you find in Chinatown. He slowly uncased a three-foot long blade from its sheath.

"Check it out," he said with a smile.

Every organ in my body rebelled against the scene. Fragmented thoughts flew through my mind. I remembered him swearing he wasn't violent and recalled Officer Ramirez's warning that there was no way I could be certain how far he'd go. I had also heard Arnon promise things would be okay, and finally, I thought of my mother, at home in our kitchen, completely unaware her daughter's mentally ill ex-boyfriend was standing a short distance away from her holding a sword, just before she was about to leave him forever.

Through the grace of the supernatural force that somehow gets us through things we can't imagine getting through, I maintained my composure and held back signs of fear. His alter ego seemed to thrive off my fear, and I couldn't risk a surge of mania while he had his hands on a weapon.

In a low, steady tone, I said, "Adam, that sword makes me very uncomfortable. I don't think you mean for it to, but it does."

"Why?" He proceeded to pose and motion with the sword as though he were fighting the air. He *wanted* me to say I was afraid.

I thought of the camera and his inflated ego. "Actually, you look really good doing that."

"I do?" he asked.

"You look like an ancient warrior or something." I caught his attention. "Here, let me take a picture. You can see for yourself." I took the camera from the table and started shooting photos as if I were paparazzi and he a famous face.

I took over a dozen pictures of him posing with the turban, the robe and the blade. Once I had convinced him he didn't scare me, I told him again that the blade made me uncomfortable. This time he returned it to the closet and pulled out a practice sword made of wood, then continued to pose. After several compliments, he asked to see the photos, and I used it as a chance to get away. I hugged him as I handed him the camera and hauled the last box towards the door.

"Hang on," said Adam. "I'm going to the city. I'll ride with you."

"Sure, okay," I said, hot-stepping it to the car, fully aware there was no room for him.

Once inside, I locked the doors and called him quickly to break the news he didn't fit.

"Okay, never mind," he said. "I'll go later."

"Take care of yourself, Adam."

He hung up with no response.

I peeled rubber away from the curb and reveled in the finality. Adam had his charger, the money he thought I owed him, and the apartment all to himself. We were no longer a couple, our ties were severed, a new life awaited me in Queens, and I was ready to put the worst behind me.

CHAPTER 18

❖

SOMEONE WISE ONCE SAID that God never burdens us with more than we can handle. With all the pandemonium of the past few months, I expected the Universe to show mercy in other ways. So far it had: My boss had let me take time off with ease, I'd found a new place to live fairly quickly, and Adam's threats had turned out to be rhetoric. My move to Queens symbolized my healing process, which in my mind meant it had to turn out right. Any bet at that point felt like a safe bet.

It was almost 10:00 p.m. when I unloaded the last box in my new Queens home. A cool summer breeze was blowing through the windows. Oliver meowed most of the night as he investigated unfamiliar surroundings. Lulu hid in a corner.

The next morning I woke sticky with sweat and found Oliver in the other room, panting heavily. Forget what God thought I could handle—if something happened to Oliver, all bets were off. Some quick research on the Internet led me to an emergency animal hospital hotline in the city. Ollie was overheating. There were two ceiling fans in the apartment but no air conditioning, and I had underestimated the impact of early August humidity. I ran to the shower, adjusted the water to a cool setting, picked up the cat and stepped in the tub with my clothes on. The water soaked Ollie's long, black fur, and he buried his little head in my neck, grateful for my love. After I dried him off, he perked right up, crisis averted. His wet fur would keep him cool long enough for me to drive to Walmart to buy an air conditioner.

I changed my clothes in a hurry and went to brush my teeth. Suddenly, a small roach crawled across the sink basin. I stepped back in shock, then turned on the faucet and washed it down the drain without much concern. This was New York City. A random bug here or there was part of life.

Schneider helped me carry the heavy air conditioner upstairs. As he installed it, we made conversation. Aside from his job as a super in three of my landlord's buildings, he also worked with a local contractor. He wore paint-stained clothing and had kind blue eyes. I could tell he found me attractive, but he never crossed the line. Once he heard the short version of how I had ended up in Queens, like most people he simply wanted to help. Before he left, I told him about the roach in my sink and asked if anyone else in the building had bug issues. Schneider said no, but that he'd come back later that day to seal up any cracks in the walls.

The first few days in a new apartment always excite me— the way each item gets a special spot that comes together to build a home. When I moved in with Adam, I had sold or thrown away most of my things, so with a handful of discount coupons, I set off to Bed, Bath & Beyond to dress my new abode. My new start felt fresher by the second, but it wasn't enough; I needed to go a step further.

A few years back, I had seen a program on a local cable channel hosted by a Buddhist monk who answered questions from viewers. Someone asked why Buddhists shaved their heads; the monk claimed it helped reduce chaos in their life. He said our hair causes unnecessary worry to look a certain way and meet other's expectations, so Buddhists often shave it off as part of their cleansing path to happiness. I knew a couple of people who had taken this type of extreme measure during dark days in their past. Most recently, in his manic state, Adam had shaved his head completely. Now it was my turn. I called my hairdresser, Antonio, and asked him to make a house call.

Calm down— I didn't go all Sinead O'Connor or anything like that. Antonio was an artist who'd always wanted to try a short style on me. I finally acquiesced. Adam was a huge fan of my long hair, which vastly contributed to my decision to snip off eight inches of it.

When Antonio finished, I sent a selfie to my mom and Deb titled, *My New Look*. They sent back compliments I needed to hear, and as the Buddhist predicted, my chaos quotient felt a little smaller.

When I finally went back to work, it strangely felt as if I had never left. People assumed I'd gone on vacation, and I didn't correct them. My professional world offered refuge from my personal hell. Adam left me alone, and my small steps forward seemed to be making headway.

On Sunday, August 3, I received a message from Joni, the double-agent neighbor from Brooklyn who had ratted me out. Her voice palpitated with concern for Adam. He had visited her apartment three times that day, and it was barely past noon. She said she had heard strange sounds through her ceiling, and that Adam didn't look well. She wanted Arnon's number to see if he could help.

A few minutes later, I received the first call from Adam since he held me at sword-point in our old living room. I declined to answer and sent him to voicemail. When I checked the message, his tone sounded friendly. He even laughed at times. He claimed he wanted to see how I was doing and to explain about the picture of Naz and the mysterious art subject I had seen on his camera the day I moved out my things. He sensed my jealousy towards the girl, told me he'd "been a good boy" and was "ready to explode down there" because he hadn't been with anyone sexually since me. He stressed the fact I had no right to question him, but he wanted to explain anyway. He also said he was planning to take a bike ride in the park with an "African friend" and wanted to invite me along since he still had my Mongoose at the Brooklyn apartment. I had left it behind along with my karaoke machine, because I couldn't fit them in the car. Adam knew both items meant something special to me, but not enough for me to brave the torture of a return visit.

"So. . ." said his digital voice. *"Give me a call. I love you. I wanna talk to you. I miss you. . . . Bye."*

My stomach dropped. Adam sounded. . .*sweet.* I had spent the last few days forcing myself to accept the idea that he and I were done, but he only thought I was keeping my distance because I was jealous. I chocked it up to another mood swing and chose to ignore him. Ignorance was a mild retaliation technique that guaranteed results—just not the results I anticipated.

By August 5, the messages were begging me to call him. He swore he still loved me and always would. He sounded soft and desperate for forgiveness. My heart burned as I listened. *I'm not angry anymore. I need to talk to you. I hate myself. Please?*

Adam hated himself? That made sense to me. Was it possible he had finally come to his senses? No. . .no, it wasn't. The rest of the message declared he would take a lie detector test to prove he hadn't been with other women. In fact, he already had it scheduled with the same officer ready to arrest me at the Seventy-second Precinct. He claimed he had forgiven me. He felt I'd learned my lesson and that he too had learned his: He didn't want to live without me. He only wanted me.

Sure, I had waited a long time to hear those words, and as with every message before it, I broke a little more. I hung up the phone and cried over the cruel trick being played on me. The man I loved still loved me back, but the context of his mind was so jumbled, it resembled a puzzle one finds in the Sunday paper. He was right about one thing. I had learned a valuable lesson, that his kindness had an expiration date that came without warning. No matter how badly I wanted to, I couldn't give in to his sweetness.

Still, the angst in his voice tore me apart. I felt like a mother forced to let her child cry as he learned to sleep through the night. I put myself in his shoes and imagined what it would feel like to reach out for someone with no sign of a response. It would kill me. What happens when one is faced with the threat of mortality? They fight to survive. Adam proved more than willing to fight dirty.

The messages continued over the course of several hours. Each time I failed to call back, his tone escalated. Instead of demands for a Macbook charger or money I owed him, he tempted me with my bike and the karaoke machine I had left behind. He mentioned he'd gotten a new job with a different brokerage. He sounded manic but able to function. It could easily have seemed like an improvement. Finally, by the afternoon of August 6, Adam said the magic words to provoke my response:

Hello, Amanda. I really don't appreciate how you're not calling me back, considering it was you and my father who made me be in the hospital for six days instead of three, makin' me lose money. But I'm with Smith Harris Real Estate, first day on the job. . . . Today's the second day—first day on the job, I closed my first deal, with my apartment, and I'm gonna be gettin' money for it next week.

Umm. . .you need to call me, because I will have Officer Billy from the Seventy-second Precinct come and pick you up, wherever you are, and make sure you never work anywhere in the United States of America again. And if you call my father I will also do that as well. So, if you don't call me, that happens, and if you call my father that happens, okay? So. . . .

And if you want to see me, if you wanna see me, which I really wanna see you, 'cause I still love you, I will always love you, I will show you the Airborne patch I got from Sergeant First Class that I could show you, because I enlisted in the military for intelligence and could show you proof of all that. And. . .

please give me a call. It's definitely in your best interest considering you attacked me and I still haven't enacted vengeance within the hands of the law, which would be having you arrested as well as serving time. And trust me, you will not have a good time in prison 'cause that place is like a zoo.

So, ya know, just please give me a call. That's all I ask. . .ummm. . .Ya know, because I do wanna talk to you and realize I—I have spared you this whole time. Ya know? And I don't wanna take—in fact I'm not going to. Just realize, I'm not gonna have you arrested. But. . .in terms of work. . . . Ya know I might, ya know, make sure the people at your work know what you really did rather than what you told them, ya know, that happened. Which was a lie. Ummm. . .so. . . . Ya know, I just tell the truth, so I'll tell the people at your work—Greg O'Grady, Beverly Saunders (i.e, my immediate Supervisor and the Vice President of Human Resources).

I'm letting them know what a great worker you are, and they'll put out a good reference for you as well, for your new job, knowin' what a great worker bee you are. Okay? Just realize I love you and I don't wanna ever do anything to hurt you or your job, but realize you physically hurt me. And. . .I have a right to enact the law, but I won't, if you call me.

Love you. . .Bye.

Fuck: That's the only word I can think of to accurately describe what I felt inside. Adam knew the names of people in key positions at my job. He had actually listened all those times I came home and told him stories, the way a girl tells her lover about her day when he asks. Just my luck, between delusions he had managed to retain the information. Then I recalled his interviews with the company months before. He had sent a thank-you letter to Beverly Saunders, which meant he had her email address. It wouldn't be hard for him to figure out the email format for any other employee he could find within the company. I had just settled back in at work; I couldn't risk the rants of a crazy man, nor could I ignore his threats any longer. I called Adam back and agreed to meet him the next day in Columbus Circle, at the entrance to Central Park. He left me a message requesting toenail clippers and some low-grade weed so he could *pick the seeds out and eat them like bird seeds since* [he] *now savored everything.*

As I approached our meeting spot by the steps, I did what I could to hide my fear. From a distance I scanned the crowd for Adam's face. When I finally spotted him, I hate to say it— he took my breath away. He was wearing a purple tank top that clung to his lean, muscular body. His suntanned skin featured his white teeth when he smiled, and his espresso eyes glistened with shades of gold in the light. I watched him exchange banter with a random stranger. His natural beauty and height-ened charm made it almost impossible to see Adam as the big, bad wolf he'd become. *Almost.*

His eyes lit up when he saw me.

"Amanda!" he gasped.

"Hi, Adam," I answered as he hugged me. It took all my strength not to completely let go and join him in La-La-Land.

"Did you bring what I asked?"

"Sure did." I handed him a tiny brown paper bag with toenail clip-pers inside.

"Did you bring the weed?"

"Sorry, Adam. I don't smoke weed anymore. I didn't have any to bring you."

It wasn't quite the truth, but I'd be damned if I'd give him any more ammo to blackmail me with. We sat down together on a nearby bench.

"I joined the army," said Adam. "See?" He pulled out a business card for Sergeant Somebody at army headquarters. It looked legit.

For the record, I consider soldiers our bravest heroes. But as much as I support our troops, I could never date a soldier. Call me selfish, but I couldn't withstand the risk of a true love going to war for months at a time with high odds of dying. I greatly admire anyone who can do that, but I couldn't. Adam knew that. I don't know if he said it to get me to try and stop him, or to prove once and for all my dream of us would never, ever come to fruition.

"If that's what makes you happy," I said. "The Iranian army or the American army?"

"Huh?" he looked confused.

"On your birthday, you said you were joining the Iranian army."

"Oh yeah," he laughed. "That was stupid. The American army."

"Well...that's good to hear."

"Ya know," said Adam, "in a few weeks you won't hear from me for a very long time."

"No?" I asked.

"I'm going to be part of an intelligence operation in Iran." He smiled proudly.

"Really?"

"Yeah. The army tested me. I scored through the roof. They want to use me on missions."

"Awesome," I said. "Sounds like you're all set."

"Yeah, but there's one more thing I need to do before I go."

"What's that?" I asked.

Adam's face grew serious. "I need to go to the Observation Deck."

A lump formed in my throat. "Why?"

"I just want to draw the skyline, so I can take the picture with me before I leave. I want some fresh air. I can go anytime I want. I just don't want to have to buy a ticket."

Work was a trigger Adam detonated as a means to control me. I apparently hadn't responded to his army comments in the way he wanted.

"Adam," I said quietly, "you keep saying you want to go to the deck, but you didn't bother to go during the entire last year I worked there. Why do you have to go now?"

"Because I *want* to!" he shouted. "Besides, I'm the reason you even work there. If I hadn't given you the confidence to stick it out when you hated it, you wouldn't be there. If I wanted to right now, I could have you fired!"

"Don't you understand that, with everything that happened, I'm in trouble there?" I figured, if I played a victim, he might take pity.

He softened only to savor the power of his influence. "You are?" He asked intrigued.

"Yes. If you show up, it could make it all worse. Why don't you go to the Empire State Building instead? I'll give you twenty dollars towards your ticket." Money was Adam's trigger.

"Okay, if you're gonna pay for the ticket, I'll go to Empire instead." He did his best not to drool over the cash as I handed it to him.

Since the moment he got sick, money had played a role in his mania. My guess was, it went mostly to drugs, but manic spending sprees are known to occur during bipolar episodes. He wore several rings and necklaces like those found on the sidewalks of Canal Street. Crack whores will suck a dead man's dick for twenty bucks, but I was nuts to think it might be enough to bribe Adam to relinquish his hold over me.

"I gotta get going," I said to Adam.

"Already?" he said.

"Yeah, I have groceries on their way. I gotta be there for the delivery." It was a pathetic excuse, but it worked.

"Okay. Well, can I see you again soon?" he asked.

"Adam, I think it's best we just leave things as is. You've got plans for a future that don't include me, and I've got to rebuild the future I planned. I wish you all the joy and success in the world, but I can't continue to communicate with you. It hurts too much to know you want to move on without me."

"I *don't* want to move on without you!" said Adam. I just can't move on *with* you in the way you want me to!"

His words struck a nerve in me, and I took his bait. "That's all well and good, but I don't have to settle for what you're willing to give if it's not what I want."

"You're such a spoiled little brat," he snapped. "You always have to have everything the way *you* want it. You're a spoiled piggy."

"Goodbye, Adam." I put my arms around him and he pulled away.

"Get off me!" he snapped.

"Good luck in the army. Don't get shot."

I left. He muttered something about me beating him to whoever was close enough to hear. I grabbed a cab back to Queens, convinced again, for some reason, I was finally done with Adam.

Yet, again, for the same reasons as before, I wasn't.

My babies ran to the door as I entered exhausted from my visit with Adam. I went to the bathroom to splash some water on my face. In my peripheral vision, I noticed another tiny roach crawling on the shower wall. It was the second one I'd seen, but still no major cause for concern. Tissues and a toilet were all I needed to squash the little bugger. After a round of clean-up in each of the rooms, I moseyed over to my computer desk to work on my story—yes, *this* story, back before I had any clue how it would end.

Steadfast and focused on words, I started typing away at my keyboard. Suddenly, Oliver darted past me from the kitchen toward a corner of the room. There I saw a centipede at least two inches long scramble for its life. I grabbed a can of bug spray Schneider had left me and hosed down the bug as if it were on fire. I started shaking. To my left I saw something move and sprayed without thought. Lucky I didn't mace myself in the process—it turned out to be a ball of fur left by Oliver as he raced for cover from *Operation Centipede*. I couldn't help but laugh at the scene, but for the rest of the evening I jumped five feet each time a dust particle fluttered my way.

I lay in bed that night unable to sleep. My legs twitched from imaginary, creepy-crawlies under my covers. My mind danced with images of Adam as Dr. Jekyll and Mr. Hyde. I thought of some poor desk jockey named Officer Billy at the Seventy-second Precinct who probably hated his job more than usual these days. I tried to watch TV, read a book, even prayed. Finally, with Lulu nestled quietly at my feet, Oliver crawled up to my pillow and curled up into a ball, his head tucked under my chin, he reached his furry little paw across my chest and rested it on my hand. He purred me a lullaby, and with the unconditional love only animals can give, I drifted off in peace.

CHAPTER 19

❖

HEY SAY TV ROTS THE BRAIN, yet so much of what I have learned over the years has come from watching scripted drama portrayed by actors. As a writer, I'm fascinated by dialog used to create the illusion of everyday life. It's easy to get caught up in, and even easier to misconstrue as reality. I'm certain that years of watching soap operas and romantic comedies contributed to my warped interpretations of love. I thought it was acceptable to break up a home for true love. I was wrong (I learned that the very hard way). No one regrets the role I played in Adam's divorce more than I do. Not a day goes by that it doesn't haunt me in some way or form.

Then again, so does Adam.

Time went on, and so did the incessant phone calls from him. When I didn't answer, he left messages. The longer I waited to reply, the angrier and more threatening they got. In one message, he claimed to have had *"the best night of his life,"* said he saw *"beautiful things he always wanted to see."* A day later, he claimed that, since I no longer wanted to be with him, he thought I should know he had cheated on me several times when we were together, often with prostitutes. He may have been crazy, but I'd say crazy like a fox. He knew exactly what to say to hurt me. He stockpiled his words like guns in an armory and used them to slowly murder my spirit. The day after that, he apologized and begged to see me. He didn't stop: He didn't even slow down. By August 14, my voice mailbox was full, jammed with messages since the ordeal began.

Television may have given me some bad habits over the years, but shows like *Law & Order* also taught me some valuable lessons. My gut told me not to delete those messages, that I might need them at some point. I decided my gut might be onto something.

Back in 2008, before I had an iPod, my Zen MP3 player came with a voice recorder. I played all of Adam's voice messages back on speakerphone and recorded them as an Mp3: the last four weeks of hell in more than forty-five minutes of audio from my former lover. I listened to each one, back to back, in the name of posterity and potential evidence. Several of them you've read here. On the actual recording, I added a few words at the beginning to explain why the recording was necessary. At the end, I described how it felt to relive all the drama in one sitting. Alone in my Queens apartment, I was standing in the kitchen; the sky grew dark as the minutes ticked by. The following is a transcript of my own words after the last message finished playing:

> *I have to tell you that listening to forty-six and a half minutes of what has happened over the past month has probably been one of the hardest things I've had to do throughout this entire process. I played these messages as a record of what [Adam] has been doing, the things that he said, his erratic behavior ...I don't know if anyone is gonna hear them. I hope to God not! I hope he just leaves me alone. I just really recorded them because I don't trust if he is gonna leave me alone and I have to delete some messages off of this phone, so I figured if I could do it this way, great.*
>
> *But whoever hears this, if anybody ever does, the one thing I gotta say is, this just really wasn't the man I fell in love with. I never thought he would... do this sort of thing. I never thought he would use everything that he's ever*

heard about anyone against them, and tell lies. I never knew this was what he was capable of. What I knew about his disorder was that he had not taken his medicine for several years, and that that was supposed to be a good thing, because he'd managed to overcome it. What I knew about bipolar disorder was that it was more of a depressive state. It was never this manic, hyper, angry state that he is in. So. . .I wasn't expecting this.

There are things that he's doing, and things that he's saying, that, if you asked me about the Adam I fell in love with, I would tell you he would never do those things or say those things. For that, I tried very hard to help him, I tried to love him. I tried to be the best woman I could be to him. But he just hated me more and more. He demanded more and more. He wanted my money. He wanted me to get him drugs. He just wanted me to do whatever he wanted, and when I would refuse, he would hate me. At one point I tried to talk to him during the phase of the nice messages you heard. Some nice messages would come after a horrible night of horrible messages, and some horrible messages would come after a nice night. Everything is just backwards with him. I don't know how to fix it. I can't, and I don't want to.

Please know that I loved this man. And I really want what's best for him. I just want him to get better. I've never before in my life watched a man who has worked so hard to get to a point, destroy everything by completely destroying all of the relationships of the people that loved him, up until this point. They say it happened before when he was younger. I didn't know him then. I only want him to succeed in life. I believed in him, and I truly saw goodness in him, at many times. I will forever have to live with what happened. I will never forget it, not a day in my life. But all I want is for him to leave me alone, and to let go of me, and not to hurt me. . .to get help. So he can someday again be the man I once knew.

Just know I loved him. But it's not him anymore.

Whatever peace I thought that speech brought me didn't matter. Deleting those messages didn't stop Adam from calling. In fact, over the course of the next few days, I would be grateful I'd listened to my gut and appreciative of shows like *Law & Order SVU* that taught me I could never be too careful.

On August 24, things took a turn for the worse. It was a hot Sunday afternoon. I had the opening shift at the deck and managed to finish a few minutes early. The trek home from the train in my suit made me sweaty. I dropped my things off in the kitchen and immediately went to change clothes. I heard the phone ring from the other room. By the time I made it back I had a new message.

"*Hey, it's me!*" said the voice. "*I'm here! At the deck. Are you working?*"

The room started to blur.

"*Yeah, I just rode up in the elevator. Now I'm here in the retail shop. Are you here? If you're here, come up and see me, okay? I love you. Bye.*"

My knees felt weak; *Adam was at the deck.* He'd raised the bar on how far he would go to get my attention. He'd made specific references, so I knew for certain he was there. I must have just missed him. I felt sick over the scene this could turn into. I pulled it together and dialed the closing manager, Don, to tell him what was going on. He knew Adam used the deck to toy with me, but none of us had ever thought he'd follow through with an attempt to threaten my job.

Don had never met Adam, so I quickly sent him a picture. He and a few other managers searched the attraction but failed to find him.

Don suggested the time had come to inform Human Resources of the situation. He said it was for my own good, and I couldn't help but agree. I hung up the phone in a state of shock and utter vulnerability. Suddenly, a roach crawled down the kitchen wall. I grabbed a nearby catalog and whacked the bug repeatedly as I shouted, "I want you *dead!*"

I'm not proud to admit I didn't just mean the bug. As much as I know I could never commit murder, I can now say I understand how a person gets there emotionally. Adam was like a monster that wouldn't go away until he destroyed everything that mattered to me. I just wanted

him to stop! I prayed for him to hunt for crack in the wrong neighborhood and end up in the gutter. I had once loved this man, and now I
was consumed by anger and hate for his lack of control and malicious
intent. The thought of filing a complaint tempted me, but I still hoped
things would go away without getting to that point.

The next day, I sat with the security guards at work and studied the
surveillance camera footage from the time frame Adam called. Since no
one had found him while he was there, we couldn't be certain this wasn't
another one of his delusions. After an hour or so he appeared on screen.
He'd told the truth; He *had* come to the deck. I watched him go from
floor to floor with a smile on his face like an actual tourist. He wore
denim shorts and a polo shirt, and had a yarmulke on his head. Aside
from the fact I knew he was out of his mind, he looked like an average
guest in the attraction. As I tracked the footage in the security office, a
group of associates from the closing team came in to get radios and cash
drawers for their shift. One girl looked surprised to see me behind the
security window.

"Amanda! There you are. I was looking for you yesterday."

". . .You were?" I asked her.

"Yes! A guy came by the shop upstairs and left something for you."
She handed me an envelope with the deck logo on it.

My stomach seized as I took the envelope. "Thank you."

"You're welcome!" She smiled, happy to complete the delivery. I,
however, felt as if she had handed me a death sentence. Like anthrax
might be sprinkled on whatever was inside.

My name appeared in large, fancy lettering across the front of the
envelope. Inside were two pieces of paper. One was a strip of blank receipt paper from the shop. Adam must have asked the girl for something
to write on. On the back of the receipt paper it read *From ADAM* in the
same fancy lettering as my name.

The second piece of paper had a different texture. It felt thick and rough, like a page torn from a sketchbook. Both sides were covered in ink, drawings layered upon each other. One side showed some type of ancient female figure, like a sphinx on all fours, but without the square head. Instead, it appeared to be my head, with a pointy, elfish ear. She centered the page and everything else surrounded her. In the bottom left corner was the figure of an ancient-looking man. He wore a tribal cloth and had an alien-shaped head. He was much smaller than the woman; everything was. The space around them was filled with smiley faces that resembled psychotic clowns. My name was written across the bottom of the page: *Amanda*. There were diamond shapes, crosses, and stars scattered among everything else. Triangles covered the page in one form or another, as a tribute to the letter A's in my name.

The other side of the paper read in large script, *I love You 4-EVER*. There was a heart drawn with Cupid's arrow aimed at it. Inside the heart Adam had written *I 4-GIVE U* and dated the picture *8/24/08*. It took time to make sense of the image. It gave me insight into Adam's current state of mind, which was nothing short of a hot mess. His artistic skill was less presidential scholar and more childlike doodle. Bipolar disorder had scrambled his brain like breakfast eggs.

Once I had actual evidence Adam had come by, I had to brave the awkward conversation with Margie in Human Resources. To this day, I marvel at the support I received from my HR department. Margie had heard her share of stories throughout her career, but never one quite like mine. I told her about Adam's threats to send emails to my bosses; she told me to start by giving a recent picture of Adam to our security team in case he tried to show up again. Threats to send emails were different than actually sending them. No harm had been done yet. *But it sure didn't take long.*

When my swing shift ended, I made my way home drained from the day. Hours of scanning security footage, followed by hours of discussion with Human Resources, had taken their toll. I left the building, headed for the subway. The phone rang in my hand. It was Adam. I had to be very cautious about how I handled him moving forward. My work would support me as long as I didn't encourage his behavior. Before I could decide whether or not to answer, he had left a message.

"Amanda," Adam said angrily, *"it's me. I'm tired of you ignoring me. I'm taking action."*

I honestly thought it was another threat to arrest me. I *wish* that had been the case.

> *I have the email ready to go. I'm sending it to Greg, Beverly, Mr. Tejada, and Officer Billy at the seventy-second Precinct, as well as Sergeant La Cortiglia in the U.S. Army and my brother Mason, Dom DelMarco. I will tell them all the truth about you. You will never work in this country again! You want to ignore me? You will see my wrath. Consider the email sent!*

Oh, dear God. Perhaps I should've returned his phone calls. Maybe I should've seen him when he asked. Had I given him drugs, he might have shown mercy. At that moment, I only knew ignoring Adam had turned out to be the wrong solution. I was about to pay for the error of my ways. He had me backed against a corner, and there was nothing I could do to stop him.

I froze on the sidewalk. My hands shook as I scrolled through my contacts for Margie's number. It was already after 8:00 p.m.; there was a chance she wouldn't answer.

"Hello?" she said.

"It's Amanda. *I think we have a problem. . . .*"

CHAPTER 20

❖

THE NEXT MORNING I AWOKE IN A PANIC. I hadn't meant to fall asleep! I'd thought, if I stayed awake, the day would never come, and I was terrified of what it would bring. I grabbed my Blackberry and instantly checked for signs of Adam's wrath. There was nothing. No missed calls or voice messages. More importantly, no new emails. For the moment, no news was good news. The sun shone bright, and I had the day off. I needed coffee.

The closest coffee shop was a ten-minute walk away, so I made my way to a little Greek place around the corner from my apartment, a tiny gem that seemed on pace with the trend but was in the wrong location. Despite the irony, I was grateful for a neighborhood place to go where they remembered my order and I could sit with my laptop to write.

The sun warmed my face at the outside table. A breeze passed every few seconds. My panic subsided as I savored the simplicity of the moment—the calm before the storm Adam had warned was coming. I wondered if he would really do it. I'd stayed up most of the night expecting he would, but perhaps that was the punishment he intended. Maybe he just wanted me in a perpetual state of fear. He liked control. The mere threat of the email was enough; he didn't actually have to send it. Maybe he would realize, before he pressed *Send*, the impact of what it would do, and the tiniest drop of sanity he had left would stop him. In that moment, amid the calm, I still had hope. Then my phone buzzed against the table.

As I read Adam's email, tingles permeated my body. Everything around me slowed down. He had finally done what he'd set out to do: addressed it to all the people he said he would, including someone with an army address, and his fellow Mason brother. He had replaced my immediate supervisor, with a New York State Assistant District Attorney.

In his letter, Adam said he felt compelled to warn all recipients that I was suicidal. He said I suffered from depression, and that I had attacked him with a knife. He demanded they do not fire me but, instead, support me as I got help, or he would reveal the secrets I had told him about my co-workers. He claimed I suffered from a *"bad case of pillow talk,"* and he knew all about the escapades that went on there. Without using direct names, he suggested knowledge of a sexual history between two high-level managers, one of whom happened to be the head of Human Resources and a recipient of the email. He claimed he was working with an assistant DA to take down a drug ring in his neighborhood. He closed with one last demand that I receive the time I needed to recover, or they would all be exposed.

Margie skipped the hellos when she answered my call. "I saw it."

"It's not true!" I told her.

"I know it's not true. Beverly has seen it." Margie added sarcastically, "She really enjoyed the part about the managers who slept together."

"What am I gonna do? Am I gonna get fired?" I asked desperately.

"No, you're not. But you need to file a formal complaint. You're protected against domestic violence, but we need to see you making an active effort to control the problem."

"How do I show that?"

"First," said Margie, "we need to meet with Beverly. Come into the city, and we'll go see her together. Then we'll meet with the head of our security department, Bob. He's a former police commissioner. Since Adam threatened you on work grounds, and via work email, we can probably file a report with one of the officers here. Bob will point us in the right direction."

With that, the decision had been made. I'd spent weeks on the run from this outcome, first in fear Adam would involve the police, then in denial I would have to. I had little choice if I wanted to keep my job (and *myself*) safe. Adam had crossed a new line, and I couldn't continue to pretend there was a limit to how far he would go. I took a not-so-refreshing sip from my iced coffee, and the sun blinded me as I walked home to prepare for a new level of confrontation. Before I left, I had burned a recording of Adam's messages onto a CD in support of my own defense.

Within an hour, I was sitting across Beverly's desk on the executive floor of my company. Margie sat off to the side for moral support. There were several minutes of silence as Beverly glanced from my eyes to her computer screen and back.

When she finally spoke, we went through the email line by line. I cringed in embarrassment when we reached the parts that implied her sexual misconduct. Rumor had it that, before Beverly left my branch of the company, she'd had a fling with my supervisor, Greg. I had never thought a bit of water cooler gossip to the man I loved would come back to bite me that way. Pillow talk was supposed to be inadmissible! Though we never acknowledged it openly, all three of us had read the email, and all three of us knew what Adam meant. I was mortified.

"You're suicidal?" asked Beverly. "Why would he say that?"

"I think he knows it's one of the worst things he could say. Or he's projecting how he feels onto me," I said.

"You pulled a knife on him?"

I shut my eyes in shame. "That was—" I struggled— "last year. We had a fight, and I got a bit too dramatic and sort of threatened myself with a knife to scare him. He keeps bringing it up as though it just happened, but it's out of context." I shifted awkwardly in my chair and muttered under my breath, "I can't believe I have to *tell* you about this."

"Why did he send it to Mr. Tejada?" she asked.

Good question. "It could be he knows he has a high position in the company. It could be that Mr. Tejada rejected him for the leasing-manager position. Right now, most of the people Adam goes after played some significant role in his life the last few years. It hit him hard when he didn't get that job." I hesitated before I asked, "Did Mr. Tejada see the email?"

"We managed to reach his assistant before he got in and had her intercept it," said Beverly.

"Thank God," I said, relieved.

"We also contacted the IT department and had them reroute any future emails from Adam to a junk folder, so we don't run the risk of him doing this again."

"That's great!" I said. "Thank you."

Beverly said very seriously, "I'm worried about you, Amanda. I've been doing this a long time, and I've seen women involved in abusive relationships, but I've never had anything like this happen."

"Me neither." I laughed nervously.

"It's not funny," she said sternly. "He could hurt you. He's already tried to hurt you by sending this email."

"I know."

"We will support you through this, but you need to officially file a report against him."

"I know," I repeated.

"I spoke to Bob," said Margie. "He's expecting us when we're done here."

"Arrest him if he ever comes back here," said Beverly. Her tone sounded faintly personal.

A few minutes later, Margie and I met with Bob Strong. He was a retired police commissioner and knew just about every cop in the city. A stout man in his sixties, he had a round belly and a thick New York accent. There in his office I once again recounted the gory details of the email and the history associated with it. He told me it was a clear case of harassment and called in an officer to take my statement. A short while later, a man in uniform was sitting with me as I told my tale a third time. I signed the paperwork, passed along the CD full of Adam's messages, and the deed was done.

"What happens next?" I asked the officer.

"Your paperwork will be given to a detective, and an arrest warrant will be issued for Adam. We'll pick him up, and he'll go to jail until his arraignment hearing, when he's informed of the charges brought against him. You'll be assigned a temporary restraining order until official charges are filed when we complete our investigation."

It was all so Ripped From The Headlines I felt nauseous. Instead of teasing kids they'll go blind when they sit too close to the TV, we should warn them it might someday become their real life.

Mid-afternoon I returned to my apartment exhausted by wheels set in motion I could not stop. I sighed deeply and brought my laptop from the desk to my recliner, where I sank deeply against the cushions. I needed to write. I flipped open the screen and rested my fingers against the keys. Suddenly, a roach crawled out of the computer, and my heart nearly stopped.

My urge was to throw the instrument across the room, but I managed to lay it gently on the floor. Calmly and sanely, I proceeded to get a tissue and flush the roach down the toilet, but afterwards I didn't feel the same. Paralyzed by the fear of what might crawl out from the crevices of everything around me, I jumped at anything that moved in my peripheral vision. I couldn't touch the computer or sit on the recliner. Home was no longer safe. I had to get out of there.

Dramatically, I called Schneider and told him the roaches had won. He promised to come by and caulk up any holes he could see while I was at my mother's for the night. I packed a small bag, fed the cats, and traipsed back through Manhattan to Port Authority, where I caught the bus to my safe haven.

The sun hovered just above the horizon when my mother picked me up from the bus stop. As we pulled in to our driveway, my phone rang. "Ms. Hirsch, this is Detective Kahn. I'm calling to let you know we arrested Adam Haddad."

". . .You did?" I could barely speak.

"Yes. He's being charged with aggravated harassment. He'll sit in lock up the next twenty-four hours, until arraignment. Then he'll be released on bail pending trial."

". . .Trial?" I asked shakily.

"Yes, assuming he pleads not guilty."

"Wow."

"Bottom line is, you're safe," said Kahn. "I'll be in touch the next few days to set up a time to take your statement."

"Okay," I said. "Thank you."

"You're welcome!" He sounded proud.

I hung up the phone and realized I just sent the man I loved to prison. The one thing I'd thought I would never do. Words, I'd thought, I would never say.

"What happened?" asked my mother as we entered the house. My sister was in the kitchen.

"They arrested Adam."

"They *did?*" asked my sister.

I filled them both in on the events, just another chapter in the soap opera of my life.

"You did the right thing," said my mother.

"I put him in *jail*."

"He put *himself* in jail," said my sister. "You had no choice. He threatened your *job*. You don't know what he's capable of."

I hated those words. I hated them because she was right. No one knew what the man was capable of. Every time I thought I did, he showed me I was wrong. There was always something more waiting in the wings with Adam.

That night I struggled to fall asleep despite my safety from threats, phone calls, and whatever else Adam had up his sleeve. I hated myself for how things had turned out, imagined the look on his face when he realized I had betrayed him. Most of why Adam pushed me so hard was probably because he never thought I would push back to such extent. We had been partners once, planned a future life together, and I had put him in jail. Somewhere, because of me, Adam was sitting in a cage.

Between waves of self-loathing, I thought about what had led me to do such a thing. He'd told my employers I was suicidal. He'd showed up unexpectedly at my workplace and left dozens of messages threatening to ruin my life. I hated him for that. I'd never thought he'd take it that far. For so long, I had been so. . .*wrong*.

A couple of days later, I met with Detective Kahn to give a more detailed statement. A decent-looking man in his early forties, he was dressed casually, in jeans. I barely knew the man yet felt confident he fully intended to help me.

"We listened to the messages on the CD," he said. "That was good thinking on your part to record them. All his threats are there."

Not sure how to respond, I thanked him.

He sensed my conflict. "Do you know what Adam means when he says he was 'mugged' on the recording?"

"I'm guessing he was out buying drugs and someone mugged him," I answered.

"That's exactly what happened," said Detective Kahn. "Do you know what he was buying?"

"Crack?" I guessed.

"Yes," he said, surprised I had guessed correctly. "He was buying crack up in Harlem, and he was mugged. I spoke with the ADA he included in his email to your company. It turns out he was telling the truth. He got a picture of the mugger, so they stole his camera."

I had no reaction. There was always some scale of truth interwoven with Adam's madness. The indisputable fact of his buying crack up in Harlem got under my skin, but I shook it off.

"What happens next?" I asked.

"Well. . . . In the next few weeks, you'll receive a permanent order of protection while we wait for trial."

"Am I gonna have to testify against him?"

"Yes. But that probably won't happen for several months. In the meantime, if he attempts to contact you in any way, he'll go to jail and the severity of his charges will increase."

"I see."

Kahn continued, "Since you live in Queens, I recommend going to Queens Family Court with a copy of the temporary order, to make sure he can't harass you at home."

"So this is only good in Manhattan?" I asked, concerned.

"No, but you'll get a faster response if you're already in their system."

"Oh."

"It can be rough over there," he warned, "but it's in your best interest to have your bases covered."

"Of course," I replied, doubtful I would follow his advice.

"That's about it," he said. "We'll be in touch with any progress."

"Thank you."

With that, it was over. I got up and shuffled out of the precinct. When I made it outside, the air had changed. It felt dead. I ambled along towards the subway and scanned the faces of strangers around me. It all felt so *different*: ugly and empty. Sure, I was safe. There would be no more phone calls or emails. Threats would become a thing of the past. So would our love and any hope I had ever had of our future. Adam and I could never come back from this. I'd sent him to jail, and he'd driven me to it. No couple could come back from it. The worst was over as far as anyone else could tell. I could move on with my life, re-cover from the trauma of his mania. For all intents and purposes, compared to the timeline of my history with Adam, recovery would be easy. It *should* have been easy. . . . *But it wasn't.*

CHAPTER 21

❖

ACCORDING TO *MERRIAM WEBSTER ONLINE*, a *phobia* is defined as "*an extremely strong dislike or fear of someone or something.*" Dictionary.com defines it as "*a persistent or irrational fear of a specific object, activity, or situation that leads to a compelling desire to avoid it.*" I feel that neither of these definitions captures the power or justice the word deserves. Truth is, only someone with a phobia can relate the experience to anyone else, and only those with phobias can truly understand the individual impact.

Type into Google, "What causes phobias?" and you'll get a slightly more in-depth answer. Several medical sites, such as WebMD.com or MedicineNet.com, identify phobias as a type of anxiety or panic disorder, classified into five general categories:

1. *Natural Environment Phobias*—Ex: *Fear of storms or lightning.*
2. *Animal Phobias*—Ex: *Fear of spiders or dogs.*
3. *Blood Injection/Injury Phobias*—Ex: *Fear of blood or needles.*
4. *Situational Phobias*—Ex: *Fear of elevators or bridges.*
5. *Other Phobias*—Ex: *Fear of choking, vomiting, clowns. . . .*

You get the idea.

None of the informational sites can pinpoint an exact cause of phobias but rather suggest that several factors may come into play when one is formed. WebMD indicates that eleven percent of the population suffer from phobias, with women twice as susceptible as men. Those with phobic family members are more likely to suffer themselves, but the majority of cases develop from simply witnessing a traumatic event that shapes future, irrational reactions in similar situations.

Up until the point we've reached in this story, I hadn't had much experience with phobias. I knew I didn't *like* bugs. Never had. If one came near me, I ran in the opposite direction. With conscious effort, I've managed to avoid bee stings and wasp bites my entire life (knock on wood). Aside from bugs, I consider myself a true animal lover and often prefer the company of my cats to that of most humans. I am fully aware of the role bugs play in our ecosystem as a necessary component of our survival.

But while I strongly disagree with this aspect of God's master plan, not liking something, and having a phobia about it, are two very different things. True to the above definitions, phobias induce an *irrational* response, both *emotional* and *physical*, as a result of a traumatic event. From that perspective, it makes sense my bug phobia didn't fully form until after the threat of Adam dissipated.

Note my emphasis above on the terms *irrational, emotional,* and *physical.* Fear on its own is bad enough, but fear magnetized to the nth degree in either of these areas I wouldn't wish on anyone.

Take my brother-in-law, George, for example. He has a fear of heights. Ironically, he also loves amusement park rides. Back in high school, we all took a trip to Great Adventure in New Jersey, and I watched what happened to him when he tried to climb six stories so he could speed down a slide on a potato sack. At the first flight of stairs, he was fine. As he progressed, it became a gut-wrenching tale to see whether he'd make it. By the third and fourth flights, he was crawling up the stairs on his knees, with one arm gripping the railing and the other secured to the step in front of him. He was dizzy, sweating, and eventually lost focus on anything other than his own fear. By the fifth flight, the entire line of strangers was invested in his success, offering supportive cheers and motivational comments. When George finally made it to the top and took his turn, he received a round of applause. He was able to get through it! Then he brushed himself off and moved on to the next thrill. For George, the thrill outweighed the fear. His adrenaline rush overcame the irrational responses he felt physically and emotionally that no one else was feeling. For that reason, he reached the top of the slide, made it down, and had fun in the process. But there's a reason why George doesn't visit amusement parks every weekend or dream of jumping out a plane.

Most people deal with phobias by avoiding the triggers associated with them. Working at the observation deck, I saw dozens of people from all over the world succumb to the same fear of heights George felt. I refunded countless tickets to grown adults who could not brave the glass-topped elevator or the view from the sixty-seventh floor, despite my assurances they were safe. They didn't care about the once-in-a-lifetime experience in New York City, or the breathtaking Manhattan lights at sunset, or the memories they would make with their family. They let the irrational fear take over and chose to avoid it altogether.

This begs the question: What happens when one *can't* avoid such fear? Some people will seek psychological help. Cognitive or situational therapy has been known to help people deal with phobic symptoms. For example, a woman with a fear of planes who has to fly across the country for her sister's wedding may go through several sessions with a therapist to simulate the flying experience. Each stage of treatment is designed to mimic safety in a similar environment. Someone with a fear of spiders may start out looking at a picture of a spider and complete treatment by actually holding a tarantula in his hands. But it's my opinion that, in order to proceed with such treatment, there must be an extreme desire to overcome the fear. People can't change aspects of themselves unless they really *want* to.

Three weeks after he was arrested, Detective Kahn told me Adam had pled guilty to Stalking in the Fourth Degree. A permanent Order of Protection was in effect until November 2010, and as long as he adhered to the terms, the charge would then be removed from his record. He was to have no contact with me whatsoever, not even via third parties or social media. If he violated any of those conditions, he would go to jail. I didn't have to testify. The ordeal was over.

When we hung up the phone, I leaned back in my chair, closed my eyes, and exhaled a deep sigh of relief. When I opened them, I saw a roach crawl across my wall. Over the last few weeks, I'd seen dozens of roaches, centipedes, and other insects throughout my apartment. I hated them. I killed them. I got past it. I had other things to worry about. Bigger things, like a psychotic love threatening my livelihood. Yet that particular bug sparked a new reaction in me: I was completely and utterly immobilized by fear.

Trauma is a tricky thing. I spent from July to September focused on the trauma Adam had suffered, indifferent to its effects on me. I'd simply played the hand I was given. I had chosen him, which meant I had chosen whatever came with him. His sickness wasn't my fault, but I felt responsible for not having seen it sooner. I felt guilty for the pain and inconvenience it had caused my family, helpless as he tried to destroy my professional and personal relationships. I hated myself for turning him in.

Emotions are fuel for the soul. When they are so traumatically distorted, consumed with stress and disdain, it creates a lasting impact on the body and mind that reveals itself over time. Trauma doesn't just go away. It lingers and thrives until it's confronted and understood. At the moment I hung up with Detective Kahn, when that one roach crawled across my wall, my trauma became a phobia.

It suddenly wasn't so simple to reach for a can of Raid. There were no more simple answers to killing that bug, the way there were no more simple answers in my life. I set out baits, patched up the holes in my apartment to keep them out, but they kept coming. *Would Adam keep coming?*

For weeks I had faith the bugs would go away, the same way I had thought Adam would eventually get better. Now that it was too late for us, did it even *matter* if he got better? The deepest love I ever shared had uprooted my life and spun me out of control. I knew nothing. My love meant nothing. I was nothing. I could hear that bug laugh at me as it moved across the wall. It told me that, no matter what I did, no matter how hard I tried, I could never be rid of the bugs in my world. They were always there, always would be. I didn't feel strong or courageous. I didn't have faith or hope things would improve. Instead, I fell into a deep state of panic I couldn't talk myself out of.

The blood rushed from my head as my stomach burned. I gasped for breath. My entire body trembled. I backed slowly away from the wall to formulate a plan of attack. My leg brushed up against a piece of furniture and *boom!* I shouted in terror, "Get *off* me!" and began scraping imaginary bugs from my limbs. I moved to the center of the room, away from walls, and marched in place to avoid bugs at my feet. I felt trapped in a bad horror movie, as if I had stumbled across a dead body in a dark room, only to turn on the light and find myself surrounded by them. I was completely irrational. A bug barely an inch long had turned me to maniacal mush.

I'd like to tell you my phobic reaction was a one-time deal. Instead, it got progressively worse. Each time I saw a bug, I ended up on a metaphorical ledge. I shook incessantly and marched in place for hours. I sobbed deeply and took dark excursions through the tunnels of my mind. I avoided bug areas like the plague and confined myself to a single wooden chair in the center of the room when I had to sit down. It took twenty minutes for me to enter my kitchen, armed with a weapon, just to feed my cats. I stopped cooking meals for myself to eliminate crumbs as potential bait. I couldn't wait to leave for work in the morning and dreaded the thought of coming home at night. Each phobic episode brought me closer to the brink of desperation. I lived in perpetual fear, unable to find peace. The bugs would always be a threat.

No one seemed to understand how I felt. They would tell me not to worry, that the bugs were more afraid of me than I was of them. They'd say, "Get *over* it! Bugs are part of life." No one took it as seriously as I did, which only made me feel worse. I felt ashamed, embarrassed. I started to question whether life was worth living in a bug-filled world.

That's when I decided to break my lease. At the end of September, I called my landlord and blamed the bugs for my abrupt departure. Then I called my mother and told her I was coming home.

God bless my family—they took me in again even though I had never consulted them about my decision. I packed up my things and took shelter in the only place I still felt secure, the only place I still felt sane. They gave me another chance to catch my breath and get my bearings.

Moving home may have felt like the sane choice, but all things considered it was anything but. For someone phobic of bugs, a move to the suburbs makes very little sense. Maybe the roaches were gone, but now there were spiders, crickets, mosquitoes, moths, and tons of other natural predators to fear. If reducing stress was my motive, it made less sense to increase my commute and invade a home already populated with three other generations saturated by their individual lives. My behavior was more that of a little girl who runs to her parents' bed after a nightmare. For a little while, I was able to sleep better at night. I thought I might heal. But as I mentioned before, one can't run from trauma. And I couldn't run from Adam.

After a few weeks, the ache returned. Emptiness caught up with me.

I hadn't heard from Adam, and those around me moved past what had happened. The adults were caught up in work, the kids caught up in school, and I began to feel like an outsider looking in on a world I wanted that was not mine to have. I did what I could to hide how I felt, kept my thoughts to myself. My family didn't need to hear any more about it. I knew they would have listened, but I also knew they felt my pain, and I couldn't bring myself to burden them any longer.

At night, I would escape for a drive around the neighborhood to feel free, let the music blare, smoke cigarettes, and cry as hard as I liked in the solitude of an abandoned parking lot where no one noticed.

One night as I sat in the dark, the pressure heavy in my chest, I screamed Adam's name so loud I thought the glass would shatter. Tears flooded in, and I screamed again. I felt my body succumb to grief as I screamed a third time.

Just as I managed to catch my breath and regain my composure, my friend Kai interrupted with a phone call. Eager to hear something that might distract me from the ghost in my head, I answered. "H-Hello?"

"Honey, it's Kai. I have to tell you something that I don't really want to tell you, but I feel like you have the right to know."

". . .What is it?"

"Adam called me."

"He *did?*" I asked. The words didn't seem real.

"Yes, a little while ago. He begged me to see if you would speak to him. He's afraid to reach out to you because of the restraining order."

"Oh, my God."

"Now, honey, you're doing so well, and I don't think you should speak to him," said Kai. "You need to move on, but I thought you would want to know."

I was in shock. I had just screamed his name to the Universe and within seconds gotten a response. "What. . .what exactly did he say?"

"He's very sorry. He's better now, and he realizes what he did to you.

He said he feels very ashamed, and it kills him that he hurt you, and he just wants to apologize."

A piece of my heart melted. A piece of me came alive inside. Then I thought about my family and how they suffered. I thought about what I had gone through at work. I thought about the bugs.

"Honey? You still there?" asked Kai.

"Tell Adam I'm happy he's doing better, and I forgive him, but I will not speak to him again." I struggled with the words, "Tell him I've moved on."

"Okay, honey. Good for you. You're doing the right thing," he assured me.

For several minutes I sat quietly in the car. For some reason, it always felt wrong doing the right thing when it came to Adam. It always seemed to hurt more than it helped. Still, I focused on what was expected of me. I was not supposed to still love this man. I was not supposed to want to be with him. I wiped away my tears, swallowed my pain, and headed home to search for a new place to live. I decided that, since I instinctively felt so discombobulated, I would trust that everyone else knew what was best. It was time to move on.

By December, I was so lost inside I couldn't find clear answers to the life questions that faced me. I relied on other people to guide me and let past memories set the foundation for my choices. Inside I felt apathetic to consequence, indifferent to pleasure or rewards. Still, I trusted my mother's assurances that everything would be okay. I dug deep inside for some remnant of the girl I had been before the last of my innocence dissolved. I thought of my apartment on Bleecker Street and the way it had empowered me as a young, independent woman when I moved there. It had been a time of hope and promise. Perhaps a return to Manhattan might symbolize rebirth. I found a decent first floor studio on the Upper West Side and set forth down another unknown road in my journey. It didn't matter what might be waiting along the way;

nothing could surpass the events on the road already traveled and the baggage I had left behind. If I could survive Adam and a bunch of cockroaches, I could survive anything.

CHAPTER 22

❖

OVER THE COURSE OF THE NEXT SIX MONTHS, the trauma of the previous two years ate away at my soul. I moved to the Upper West Side with the best of intentions. I quit smoking and devoted six days a week to exercise. Scenic bike rides, and runs along the river, gave me refuge from the war I fought within. My favorite runs were in the chill of winter, when the cold air pierced my lungs slightly. Something about the sting I felt reminded me I had survived. As the pavement passed under my feet, I knew I had kept going.

My co-workers were my friends by day, but I made no effort at a social life by night. I worked, and I worked out—end of story.

After a few weeks, loneliness returned, and my in-between hours were filled with should've–would've–could'ves in my mind. Some days I missed Adam, other days I hated him. All days I still loved him. Other men didn't interest me. Adam was the only one I cared about. The idea of dating someone else felt like a betrayal, not just physically, but to our memory as a whole. To the sacrifices I'd made for him, the secrecy I had lived in, and the integrity of the love I'd promised him. I had played the hand I had been dealt and lost. All that remained was endless pain pumping through my limbs with each scarred beat of my heart.

By spring the bugs returned. (Seriously, exterminators should hire me as a future-business medium.) Put me in any apartment, the bugs followed. I was the Pied Piper of cockroaches, centipedes, and now. . . *ants*.

Needless to say, it was a repeat of what I had gone through in Queens. I cried, sobbed, marched in place, gave up cooking, obsessively cleaned, and dreaded the thought of being home. Soon I dreaded everything, including my own existence. My head wasn't right.

I again turned to the only people who seemed to understand me at times when I couldn't: my family. They offered love and support, but this time they refused my plea to come home. I could tell they were tired of my impulse decisions affecting their lives, and I needed to act like the grown up I was. The bugs had transformed me into a scared little girl trapped in a big girl's body. I tried to tough it out, but any fight I had left in me waned. My family felt like the only answer. If I couldn't live with them, I at least wanted to be close by. After the last army of ants infiltrated my living room, I wanted out of my life. Since that wasn't an option, I chose to get out of the apartment. I was done with New York living. Once again I turned to Craigslist for answers.

Enter the great state of New Jersey (the most underrated one I know). The rents were cheaper, the apartments bigger, and the commute still tolerable. I planned to save a few hundred a month on rent and put it towards the purchase of a car. That way, I'd have the freedom to visit my family anytime I chose. A half-hour ride for Mom's rice and beans on any night of the week brought me comfort. I didn't need to live with them to feel safe; I just needed to know I had access to a safe zone whenever I wanted. For nine hundred dollars a month, I found a fully renovated studio in Weehawken, a town I knew little about. The ad boasted a fifteen-minute bus ride to Port Authority, and compared to the sixteen hundred and fifty dollars I paid on the Upper West Side, it seemed like a no-brainer. I set up a viewing and signed a lease the next day.

I applaud my effort to gain control over my out-of-control life, but in reality I was too far gone emotionally to make any big decision. My head was consumed by devastation and regret. I wasn't exactly capable of thinking anything through. The broker said Weehawken was the next Hoboken, and buses to the city ran 24/7. I didn't think about the four crappy flights of stairs that led to the apartment or what the neighborhood had to offer. I thought about the fully renovated space beyond the door. The cabinets were new, the walls freshly painted, and the appliances gleamed. Bugs seemed unlikely. That was enough for me. At the end of May 2009, I was packed and ready to leave the past behind yet again. Adam and I had no memories in New Jersey. Perhaps I had finally outsmarted his ghost.

A few days before the move, as a means of closure, I Googled Adam's name one last time before letting go completely. I often searched him on the Internet to make sure he hadn't been hurt or arrested. I'd never had any luck with the searches before—just the usual LinkedIn, People Search pages would pop up, or old real estate listings Adam posted way back before any of this had happened.

This time, I found an ad for a gym pass with his name on it.

At first I did a double take. I figured it was an old posting from back when we worked together, or some type of wishful thinking playing tricks on my eyes. But it was a different gym, and the date of the posting too recent. I had not seen or spoken to Adam in eight months, and according to Google, he worked a mere two subway stops away. I quickly shut my laptop, as if it would erase the imprint of what I had seen. My emotional scale played its tune through my mind. Sure, I was happy Adam was well enough to maintain a job at an upscale Manhattan gym. Then I loathed him for moving on without me. I needed a bike ride to clear my head.

Somewhere around Seventy-ninth Street, I stopped and gazed east towards the city. Adam was out there, among a sea of people. My stomach churned. Maybe it was a different Adam Haddad. Maybe I had put myself through anguish for nothing. There was only one way to find out. I checked the time on my phone. It was late enough to safely bet I would reach his voicemail. My shaky fingers dialed the numbers in the Craigslist posting from memory; I almost froze when the front desk girl answered the phone.

"Thank you for calling Solstice Fitness. How can I help you today?" answered a sweet, cheery voice.

"May I speak to Adam Haddad, please?"

"Oh, I'm so sorry. Adam has left for the day."

Thank God, I thought. "May I have his voicemail?"

"Certainly!" She sounded pleased to help.

The call transferred, and my blood pressure rose slightly with each ring.

Hello, you've reached Adam Haddad with Solstice Fitness. I can't take your call right now. Please leave your name and number, and I'll get back to you as soon as I can. Have a nice day.

There was no doubt about it; I recognized his voice from the first word. Adam was alive, well, and working on the Upper West Side. I mounted my bike and peddled like the wind towards my apartment. God only knew how long he had been this close to me, but with only three days before my move to Jersey, I was terrified of what could happen. For the next seventy-two hours, I skulked through shadowed streets, hidden by hoods and sunglasses like a CIA agent.

On June 1, I filled a U-Haul with my belongings and drove down Broadway towards the Lincoln Tunnel. I passed Solstice on my right and struggled to see any sign of Adam beyond the glass. It took a few trips back and forth from the city to complete the move. Each time I purposely took Broadway with bated breath as I passed Adam's location. When I failed to see him, I felt an unwelcome combination of gratitude and disappointment.

It only took a few days in New Jersey to realize I had made yet another bad decision. My rent might have been lower, but in reality you get what you pay for. The neighborhood hailed as "the next Hoboken" currently more resembled the Bronx. Most residents didn't speak English, and my Spanish was broken at best. The fifteen-minute commute varied widely dependent on tunnel traffic. Every other restaurant cooked fried, greasy food, and when I went running, most people stopped to see if I was being chased. Each time I waited for the bus to the city, I stared across the river in thought of Adam. We had been so close to each other without even knowing it, and now I felt so far away. I tried to tell myself it was for the best, pretended I was better off without him, but the pain inside lingered. A constant hopelessness saturated my spirit. There was no pride in moving past him, only despair.

By now, you probably know enough about my personality to call me a Believer. While at times such a trait can be a flaw, in many ways I consider it a blessing. Change doesn't scare me as much as the average person, and I deem the birth of even the strangest ideas as attainable realities. My mother raised me with a perpetual faith that things ultimately work out in the end, no matter how impossible the journey.

When I was eighteen, during my freshman year of college, I read my first self-help book, *The Seven Spiritual Laws of Success,* by Deepak Chopra. It had been only a year since my Grandpa Hector died, and I found myself surrounded by new faces on a Connecticut campus with everyone who knew me best miles away. For the first time, I felt truly lost. Chopra introduced me to the power of positive thinking, and since then, the study of the metaphysical mind has fascinated me. During many low points over the years, I turned to this type of thinking to navigate my cluttered path. Books and movies like *The Secret* and *What the Bleep Do We Know* taught me that our minds have the power to shape our destiny, to move us from dark to light. It wasn't until I moved to Weehawken I realized our mind also had the power to shift us from light to dark to *very dark.*

Apparently, it's a myth that houseflies throw up on everything they land on. In truth, they excrete saliva prior to feeding that helps their digestive process. Instead of imagining fly puke on every surface the pesky bugger lands on, you can rest assured it's more like fly drool. And don't worry; flies don't feed every time they land, only when they're hungry. Unfortunately, it's also a myth that flies spread disease through feeding. Contamination is actually spread when they land. Their feet touch everything, from manure to road kill to your burger. If you ever watched a fly land on some food you chose to keep eating and, the next day, felt like Jeff Goldblum in an experiment gone horribly wrong, it's not because the fly ate your burger. It's because you also ate manure and road kill.

By July 2009, it wasn't the new, unimpressive neighborhood that brought me to my darkest place yet. It wasn't the lack of people who could understand me when I spoke, or the fifteen-minute city commute that was more like an hour. It wasn't the four flights of stairs I had to climb to my apartment or the perpetual disconnect I felt from the universe.

It was the flies.

Though I may have made a less-than-perfect decision by moving to Weehawken, the apartment, as I have said, *was* brand new. The appliances had never been used. The windows had screens, and a piece of me felt safely free from my phobia—until one day I came home from a swing shift at work and found a fly in the apartment. By then, there was no such thing as letting a bug live once I discovered it. I didn't care if it took hours, I would not rest until I was sure the bug was destroyed. Flies were smart and quick, but I was determined and terrified, unable to go on for any length of time in coexistence. I had new tactics for this type of combat that required a magazine and a can of hairspray. The spray would stiffen the wings of the bug and make it unable to fly. Then I'd clobber it with the magazine. It was a master plan for the bug-hunter I'd become, and this fool of a fly had no idea what awaited it.

Lulu, Oliver, and I took up positions at various angles within the apartment, although I think they were more in it for themselves. Within a few minutes, the fly buzzed past me and landed on the wall. I jumped in, sprayed profusely and watched it struggle to the ground. Then I smacked the shit out of it with the magazine and scooped up its body with the pride of an Indian who had just taken a scalp. I went to bed that night feeling confident. Maybe my situation wasn't ideal, but Adam was gone, the fly was dead, and I was back in control.

The next morning I had the day off and awoke to the sun shining through my blinds. The corners of my mouth shifted towards a smile as the blue sky came into focus beyond the window slats. The brief moment of contentment came and went, though I remember it in slow motion, like the start of an avalanche on an icy, snow-capped mountain: subtle movement followed by complete, unyielding destruction.

At first it looked like a spot of dirt on the window, until it moved. Then I realized there were actually two of them. Two flies were pressed between the glass and the blinds of my window. Suddenly the sunshine didn't matter. Nothing mattered. I had killed one fly, and two had appeared. It was the same as taking one step forward and two steps back. The flies were not just insects that happened upon my apartment, they were a symbol of everything negative and dark in my world. I couldn't control the *bugs*. I couldn't control *my life*. I couldn't trust new surroundings to keep the bugs *away*.

Instead, I grew to believe I could never escape them. The darkness would follow me wherever I went. I was plagued with bugs and cursed with darkness.

I spent the length of the day hunting them down, but hunt them like a shattered warrior I did. By 3:00 p.m. there were five fewer flies in the world, and I spent my day off shaking, crying, and cursing God. A combination of fear and imagination led me to think these bugs had materialized from my thoughts. As soon as I felt confident I had killed the last one, another appeared. There were no open windows or doors. There was no explanation of why it was happening. *It had to be me.* I was wrong, dirty, and deserved punishment. I was shit. I was road kill, and the flies had come to gather at my carcass. In complete hysterics, I called my property manager and told him I couldn't handle the situation anymore.

He was a young guy at an age where any screaming woman made him panic. He tried to console me and immediately called the super, but unless the super was also a priest prepared to exorcise demons, I knew the flies would return.

It took several desperate calls before the super finally appeared that evening. Together we searched the apartment and discovered a large hole that surrounded a pipe leading to the other units. We tracked the pipe to an apartment below mine, recently vacated and due for renovation (*due* for renovation being the operative term). Clutter and filth were scattered across the apartment floor. Whoever moved out had certainly forfeited his security deposit. Several flies were buzzing through the air around the mess, quite obviously forming search parties for the friends they had lost earlier that day when they slipped through the pipeline and landed in my world.

"Oh, boy," said Juan the super in a thick Spanish accent. "Dass no good."

"No, it isn't."

"Don't worry. I fix!"

"Today?" I asked him.

"No, no, no. Tomorrow."

I'm not sure what look I gave him, but within a few seconds he had agreed to temporarily patch the hole in my place with cardboard until he had a chance to get the materials he needed for a more permanent solution. After a few bug-free hours, I managed to succumb to fatigue and fall asleep.

The next day was July 4. In honor of the anniversary of Henry Hudson's voyage to New York, the Macy's fireworks were set to go off on the west side of the city instead of the east. I volunteered to work at the deck that night for my chance at a great view. Around 6:00 p.m., my co-workers and I took a dinner break and ordered in some Mexican.

Towards the end of my meal, I felt a slight itch on the bottom of my right wrist. A few moments later, I felt one on the back of my left knee. "That's weird," I said. "I feel like I just got bit by a bug in two totally different areas of my body."

"Oh, jeez," said my co-worker Frank. "You and your bugs. You're imagining it."

We finished our meal and went for a walk-through of the deck. As we stopped to talk with some associates, I felt another bite near my waist, on my right knee, and on the inside of my left arm.

"Okay, I'm not *imagining* this!" I said as I scratched. "There is a bug in my clothes biting me."

My very handsome, very wise co-worker Don looked at me with pity in his eyes. "You really think there's a bug crawling that quickly through your clothes, biting you in different spots? Like it's the *magic bullet of mosquitoes?*"

"I'm *serious!*" I shouted.

"C'mon, Amanda," he said dismissively. "Enough with the bugs."

I figured he was probably right, but I decided to go to the ladies room and strip off my clothes just to be sure. As I unbuttoned my pants, I saw a large raised blotch on my stomach. I couldn't imagine what bug had found me. As I continued to strip off the layers of my polyester blend suit, I saw welts all over my body. My co-workers were right. It wasn't a bug. I had broken out in hives.

Aside from some issues with pollen in spring and fall weather, I don't suffer from allergies. I'd never had such a reaction before. I quickly dressed and ran to Don to show him my arm. He immediately sent me to the store for some Benadryl. It was a humid evening in July, and with each step I took, my suit brushed agonizingly against my skin.

The antihistamine enabled me to continue my shift and enjoy the fireworks, but the welts didn't entirely disappear. The next day, I saw my doctor, who had no idea what had caused them. He said there was no way to find out without going through a series of allergy tests with a specialist, and even then, the results might not accurately explain why they appeared.

"Have you been under any severe stress?" he asked.

Was he kidding? "Um. . .yeah, you could say that." I reminded him of what had happened with Adam.

"Well, *that's* more than likely what caused it. Continue to take the Benadryl, and set up an appointment for some testing, but most importantly, try to relax. It will go away on its own."

For the next week, Benadryl was my best friend. The hives came and went for seven days before they left for good with no scientific reason why. Afterward, I hoped to feel relief. Instead, I felt as if the hives had reflected the damage to my psyche and left invisible welts as permanent reminders of the traumas I had suffered. I felt incomplete, broken, and defeated. Fear dominated my every step, every choice. Sunlight began to annoy me. I yearned for darkness. I walked the streets and fantasized about stepping in front of a bus. I figured I could make my family understand that was the only real way to stop the pain. Then I thought about Oliver and Lulu and how they would never understand why their mom had just up and abandoned them. In more ways than one, more times than I can count, those cats saved my life.

On July 12, I hit the breaking point. I started crying and couldn't stop. I don't remember why. Not one thing had specifically happened to cause me to crumble. It was just time. A year of trauma finally caught up with me, and somehow I ended up at the bottom of the avalanche. I felt the walls of my apartment start to close in on me, couldn't focus on anything but my own sadness. I didn't want to call my family and give them a chance to tell me that it was all in my head and time would heal me. I wanted everything to *stop*. all the noise, all the memories, all the oxygen going in and out of my lungs. I cried so hard I almost passed out. When I finally felt ready to find a knife or some bottle of pills, I heard a voice in my head ask for help. Then I remembered a story my co-worker Don had told me about a period in his life when he lost his entire immediate family in a single year, and the struggle he had gone through to deal with it. Don had my utmost respect. Though I hated to appear weak, I had nowhere else to turn. I called him. "It's Amanda," I sobbed.

"My God—what's wrong?" he asked, concerned.

"Remember when you told me how you went through that very dark period in your life?"

"Yes."

"Well," I sobbed, "how did you get through it?"

"Through lots and lots of therapy," he said.

I laughed a little. "Really?"

"Absolutely!" said Don. "It took some time, but it was the best money I ever spent. I highly recommend it."

When the call ended, I dug through my employee papers for the phone number to a crisis hotline that would talk me down off the ledge and help me find a therapist for the long term. A woman answered and, for an hour, listened to my problems while I cried them out on my end. She understood how I felt and assured me she would help me find someone to speak to. That night I felt better as I drifted off to sleep, at least willing to see what the next day offered.

When I woke up the following morning, I realized it had been a year to the day since Adam had had his break and kicked me out of the apartment. With heavy heart, I managed to drag myself out of bed despite the burden. I spent most of the day at home before I managed to brave a trip to the city for my favorite cardio class. The entire ride in, the air felt stale and false. My life had no purpose. Eye contact made me queasy; couples in love disgusted me.

The closest subway exit left me at the north side of Union Square, engulfed by a sea of people who were managing to move on with their daily lives in a way I no longer could. I meandered south toward the gym, each step heavier than the next, as if I was trudging through mud or fresh cement. A bus passed on my right, and, again, I wanted to be underneath it.

I can't do this, I thought. *I can't do this. Not for one . . .more. . .minute.*

Then it hit me. It wasn't that I couldn't go through life for one more minute. It was that I couldn't go through life *without Adam. He* was what I missed. He was what I *wanted.* My true love had healed, and I had let everything that happened, and everyone else in the world, convince me to stay away from him. But this was *my life.* I was the one who suffered the loss, and I was the one who dealt with the consequences. The others were casualties of my war with Adam's mental illness and the power of a love that somehow kept us bonded. No one would ever be able to relate to my pain except him. Stepping in front of a bus wasn't my last choice to stop the pain. There was one more option I knew would cure it.

I reached for my phone and thought of all the people that wouldn't approve. Then I thought of myself. I thought of what I had gone through the last year and what my phone call might achieve. For me, it was a life-or-death choice. I chose life . . .and dialed. My heart pounded as the front desk transferred my call.

"Hello, this is Adam. How can I help you?" It was the moment of truth.

"Hi, Adam, It's Amanda," I said. There was a long pause.

"Amanda? *Is it. . .really you?*" he asked.

"Yes," I answered.

"Oh, my God!" He burst into tears. "I can't believe it's you! I'm so, so sorry for what I did to you!" He sobbed.

I instantly broke down in the middle of the park. *"Are you alright?"* I asked. "Are you okay?"

"I miss you so much, you have no idea! I love you so much," he cried. "I wanted to call you, I tried to reach you through Kai to apologize." He sounded desperate to say as much as he could in case he never spoke to me again.

"I miss you too," I replied, in tears. "I haven't been able to move on. I haven't been with anyone."

"Neither have I!" he exclaimed. "I can't believe you're on the phone. I swear I have done nothing but want to kill myself since I hurt you. I get up each day thinking it will be my last. Hang on. . . ." He took a second to close the door to his office.

"You're at work," I said when he returned. "You need to calm down."

"I don't even care. You reached out to me! I'm talking to you! I was afraid I would never speak to you again, that I would never get the chance to truly apologize to you for what happened. I was afraid you'd tell the police if I called, but I wanted to speak to you so bad!"

It was Adam. *My Adam.* The monster was gone. The medicine had worked, and the man I loved was there again. We took turns and re-counted our misery over the last year without each other.

"I would cry out for you all the time," he went on. "Just shout out your name." So many times I had done the same.

He eventually asked to see me, and I instantly agreed. "Can I see you tonight?" I asked, unwilling to waste another moment. We agreed to meet at Solstice when his shift ended.

"I love you so much, Amanda," he whispered. "Thank you *so much* for seeing me."

I smiled. "I love you too, Adam. I'll see you at seven."

We hung up the phone, and instantly I felt different. The layer of pain that had hardened over my skin began to crack and peel away. The clouds dispersed; warmth ran through my body. Nothing bothered me. The sunlight no longer blinded me, and young couples in love gave me a sense of hope for the future. The ordeal was over. Adam missed me as much as I missed him. He still loved me as much as I loved him. Balance to my universe had been restored, and I finally knew things would be okay. I checked the time and realized I had over an hour to kill before we met. My cardio class had already started. To compensate for the lost workout, I decided to walk from Union Square to the Upper West Side to see him. I was a girl on a mission to reclaim lost love. Nothing was going to stop me.

CHAPTER 23

❖

T HERE ARE MOMENTS IN ALL OF OUR LIVES worthy of legend. Whether you're a gold medalist who wins a race by a tenth of a second or a little boy who hits the winning home run to save his little league game, these moments remain emblazoned in our minds forever, clear as crystal—moments of pure glory that carry us through our darkest days, to remind us that true joy lingers in the cracks of our daily chaos, waiting to reward us. I have never hit a home run, nor will I ever bring home the gold, but I've had my share of small miracles along the way. None of them compare to my reunion with Adam.

From the beginning, my connection to him had always seemed a little "out of this world." I guess that's what happens when you feel something for someone you've never felt before. Add in a few strange coincidences here and there, and soon you have a meant-to-be recipe that can skew your most rational thoughts. Love can be interpreted a million ways, and often it's not until a relationship has run its course that we realize it was entirely different than we once thought.

Believe it or not, I got a dose of this on my walk to see Adam. As the fates would have it, I bumped into my ex, Sean, when I reached midtown. He was hosting at a restaurant I passed, and we took a moment to catch up. Sure, it surprised me to see him. I hadn't been in touch with him in four years, and in typical Amanda fashion I assumed our chance encounter had some deeper meaning. How often do you bump into one ex while on your way to reunite with another?

As I spoke to Sean, I discovered not much had changed with him. He was still a struggling actor in New York City, working day jobs to pay the bills. It was nice to see he was doing okay and share small talk about our lives, but one very important fact struck me: I loved Sean. I wanted him to be happy and successful. But I was absolutely fine not being part of it. That had never been the case with Adam.

The thought of Adam not being in my life made me physically ill and mentally tortured. I had spent two years living in secret for the chance to go public as Adam's true love. That fact alone should've made me reflect on my own sanity rather than spend all my time concerned about Adam's. But that wasn't what I felt in my heart. Something about Adam cut to my core, and his sick mind became the poison of my heart's desire. I'm sure you may not understand why I made the effort to re-unite with Adam. I often ponder that question myself. My answer is always the same: *I loved him,* in a way I never had before, and for me that was enough.

Perhaps, growing up, my own parents had influenced me. My father was a good man but not necessarily the one I'd have chosen for my mother. Their personalities and interests didn't always mesh. My father had a selfish side, while my mother perpetually gives. I saw this clearly at a very young age, yet they managed to make it work. They showed a unique loyalty to each other that withstood even the toughest challenges. After a fight, they always eventually made amends. They lived their tra-ditional vows until the very end, and to this day, more than fifteen years after my father's death, my mother remains faithful to his memory. I guess that, however warped they seemed along the way, I wanted the same thing—a love not everyone could understand but that made perfect sense to us.

When I saw Adam again, I felt complete forgiveness wash over my body, another new thing that had never happened to me before. I knew that emotions like anger and resentment ate away at us inside, but I had never managed to master the art of true forgiveness. If someone wronged me, they deserved to pay. Karma would get them. Yet when it came to Adam, who had wronged me in unfathomable ways, I found it surprisingly easy to see past his actions. He had been sick. Had he gotten sick with cancer or been paralyzed in an accident, I would have been there for him. How could I view a chemical imbalance in his brain as any less valid? At least we knew how to regulate his sickness. We knew high levels of stress or drug interactions were triggers. We knew medication, therapy, healthy eating, lots of rest and exercise, could restrain these triggers. When compared to cancer or paralysis, bipolar disorder seemed manageable, and if we both truly loved each other, we would both be willing to do what it took to thrive.

When I finally made it to Solstice Fitness and Adam caught my eye through the glass doors, he ran outside, picked me up in his arms, and spun me around like a princess in our own Grimm fairy tale. He had gone from hero to villain and back to hero again. Who doesn't love a happy ending?

There's a reason why we don't hear how Snow White lost touch with the Dwarfs after she and Prince Charming settled down. Nor do we hear about the PTSD Sleeping Beauty suffered from her nightmares while under the witch's evil spell. The truth is, real life isn't about happy endings. It's about good times and bad. We can only hope to have more good than bad, but when you love someone with a mental illness, it's acutely harder.

It didn't take much for Adam and me to pick up where we left off, despite the opinions of family and friends. Within two months we were living together again. Two months later, I awoke one night in October from a dream and found myself immersed in another nightmare. See, I had somehow convinced myself that the actual episode was the worst that could happen. How could it get worse than him wanting to see me raped in prison, or his attempt to get me fired? Yet there I was at 2:30 a.m., about to learn that everything I had gone through was just the tip of the bipolar iceberg. A whole new type of hell awaited in the aftermath.

Adam's side of the bed was empty. I had no reason to question where he was, but a voice in my gut told me to take notice—the same voice I had silenced for so many years when it came to Adam, the one I'd ignored the day I abandoned the West Village for Brooklyn, and ignored when Adam cried to me in the shower or when he began singing Hebrew prayers and staying up till all hours painting. It was the voice that screamed at me a few weeks after we reunited and I found a small, plastic straw used for snorting cocaine in the pocket of his jeans, but that Adam had dismissed as a lingering remnant in an old item of clothing long forgotten.

My eyes adjusted, and I saw a glow of light coming from the bathroom in the hall. No big deal, except the voice told me to get up and go open the bathroom door, without question. As I approached, somewhere inside I knew what I would find, but I didn't know how to take the first step.

Then I heard the sound of a lighter flick, and my body took over.

I pushed open the bathroom door wide without knocking. There sat Adam on the toilet, boxers at his ankles, crack-pipe and Bic in his hand. A thick liquid of smoke dancing from the glass to his lips, and the sight of my face did not prevent him from inhaling deeply. Without considering our differences in size and strength, I instinctively smacked everything out of his hand. The lighter and pipe flew in different directions; my hands were shaking as adrenaline consumed me.

". . .*Hey*-" said Adam slowly trying to stop me, high as a kite. "Don't,

Amanda, just let me finish this one hit."

"What the fuck are you *doing*?" I cried. *"How can you be doing this?"*

He reached for his boxers, and a tiny plastic bag with white crystalized powder fell to the floor. In the style of a classic Western, we glanced in slow motion at the drugs, then at each other, before each of us sprang into action at quick draw pace to secure the goods: The drugs motivated Adam to find his strength through his haze, and within seconds I was wrestling with his demons, as though somehow love acted as an emotional steroid that empowered me to think I could conquer all. But when the crack-dust settled, I had not vanquished anything. Adam was simply too high to fight back. In brief, intermittent moments when he found the lucidity for words, he didn't apologize for lying or risking everything we had sacrificed and suffered through to be together. He simply asked me to *let him have the drugs.* Though I never gave in, I stayed up with him the entire night until he sobered up. The next morning, we agreed to try counseling. I couldn't hide from who Adam was anymore; I had taken him back. Now I had to take everything that came with it. We needed professional help, not only to get over everything that had happened, but to learn how to cope moving forward.

More often than not, a manic episode is followed by a severe bout of depression and shame for what was done during the episode. As much as loved ones may forgive such actions because the person wasn't in their right mind at the time, the person who was sick struggles to move on. In Adam's case, he claimed he couldn't get past the shame of what he'd done to me. He could never understand why I had chosen to be with him and stand by his side no matter the consequence. According to our therapist, Adam felt unworthy of such love and chose to punish himself by smoking crack, and setting me up to catch him.

His plan worked. Over the course of the next three years, I caught Adam every few months in one way or another. If I didn't actually catch him with pipe in hand, I'd find used pipes and empty crack bags hidden in his drawer.

One time, he never came home. He never called. I spent the entire next day on the phone with hospital emergency rooms, worried sick he had been hurt. I filed a missing person report with the local police. He eventually called late in the evening to tell me he had felt suicidal on the train platform and decided to check in to a hospital instead. They had taken his cell phone, but it was okay because he'd met a guy in the hospital who could verify his story. . . . *And I stayed.*

Why did I stay? Because I couldn't bring myself to admit that, after everything we had been through, we weren't meant to be. I refused to admit defeat. I loved Adam with my entire being and had given up way too much to let it amount to failure. In the meantime, I reduced my self-worth to nothing by allowing a sick man, with no real commitment to the sanctity of his mind or our love, play Russian roulette with our lives.

Adam figured if he stayed on his anti-psychotic medicine, it counteracted any triggers from the crack. Whenever I saw a pipe, I crossed my fingers and prayed his demons would stay away. For the first year or so, he expressed remorse when I caught him. I threatened to leave, and after a few hours he showed up with a stack of AA and NA meeting brochures. I went with him a couple of times. I felt somewhat guilty myself—I mean, I didn't have a drug or alcohol problem, but there I was, surrounded by strangers who all thought I was one of them. On more than one occasion, their stories brought me to tears. So many of them had hit rock-bottom and survived stronger than before. *I admired them.*

It gave me hope for Adam, until I realized he had never gotten a sponsor and lied about going to meetings. The lies were the worst part. I caught that man in more lies than I could count—from why it took him two hours to come home from the corner store, to why he hadn't gotten to wash the dishes as he said he would. I felt as if I was always asking Adam, *"Why?"* and that whatever bullshit he spewed always amounted to *"Just because."*

So why, again, didn't I leave? It was. . .complicated. I didn't have any savings, my credit was shit, and I certainly couldn't go home again. Don't get me wrong, my family didn't disown me when I went back to Adam, but there was a clear sentiment of "You made your bed, now you lie in it." So it felt easier to live with the devil I knew than face my fears of the unknown. That's the thing, though, isn't it? *I never really knew Adam.* I knew what he let me see, and he kept showing me more and more of his true self along the way; I just refused to accept it. The love I had once felt for him became a distant memory, and sometimes I watched him sleep at night with a look of disgust upon my face—the same look I saw each time I glanced in the mirror. When someone you love and trust turns out to be the worst thing that ever happened to you, it's easy to stop recognizing yourself. I had no idea how I'd let things get so far.

Each time Adam lied, a piece of my soul withered away, because, for every lie he told, in the same breath he told me he loved me. He cushioned the blow with words of love. Eventually, I became conditioned to think the two went hand in hand. Often the emotional contradiction led me to a tantrum. I'd have fits of crying rage and sometimes even hit him. I'm certainly not proud of that. At the time it was the only way I could think to express my pain. I wanted to hurt him the way he hurt me, but the quickest way to lose a fight is to let it get physical. Adam would look me in the eye and swear he was clean with a crack-pipe still warm in his pocket. Still, any physicality on my part led to his instant vindication.

By August 2012, we knew we needed to separate. Neither of us wanted to break up, but living together was killing us slowly. We spent more time fighting than not, but one particular fight too many, followed by one lie too great, sealed our demise. I can't tell you what the fight was about, only that nothing memorable had caused it. We had become so accustomed to fighting, we had stopped needing a reason why. I remember us watching TV in our bedroom, and then I remember being in a rage. One of our usual—but as it was happening, it felt different. It felt unimportant and yet absolutely necessary at the same time, petty and yet monumentally significant. When it ended, and whatever last irreparable, hurtful comment was exchanged, we saw something different in each other's eyes, something warning us we had reached a point of no return. We had broken whatever we once had, but we didn't speak of it at the time. We just did what most dying couples do and retreated within.

The death of a relationship so often resembles the end of a life. The same way a terminally ill patient often spends a day or so in remission just before passing on, a couple may find a semblance of spark they once had for each other as some last-ditch effort to see if any truth between them remains.

The next day, I apologized to Adam for allowing whatever small thing had occurred to escalate to the point it had. In that moment, when I approached him as he sat on our bed, I saw him as a prism comprised of dark shales reflecting what we had become, speckled with hopeful glimpses of what we'd once been. I saw the big brown eyes and dimples that had caused my head to tilt when I first saw him eight years before. I thought of how it felt when we used to kiss. And with every bit of love I had left for him, I sincerely apologized.

Adam's eyes softened and he looked at me like he had something to say.

"What is it?" I asked sweetly.

This became a *Choose Your Own Adventure* moment for Adam, and as my choice had sealed my fate so many years ago, his too would do the same.

Adam's eyes lingered with mine long enough to show me he too saw the prism of our love when he looked at me, but then he looked away. "Nothing," he said with a nervous smile. "I. . .uh. . .booked a trip to visit my mom in Miami this weekend. When we had our fight I thought it might be a good idea to get away."

"Oh," I answered, taken aback.

"I would cancel it, but it's not refundable," he went on.

"No, of course! Go see your mom. It will be good to get away," I said, once again taking Adam at face value. "Just please forward me a copy of your itinerary, so I know where you'll be."

By that Friday morning when Adam kissed me goodbye, I had yet to see his travel plans. I told him to call me when he landed. He called me later that night, around 10:00 p.m., and told me he had settled in safely and would be seeing his mom and step-dad in the morning. I asked him to call me when he woke up. When morning came without word from Adam, I called his cell and heard an international ring tone on the other end. At that moment, my inner voice, a now trusted guide, spoke clear as crystal: *Adam lied, and he's in Jamaica.*

Why Jamaica, you ask? Because Adam loved drugs, and Jamaica had them. He had visited many times and knew the island well. We had been there together once, but he had been there several times before. After eight years, I knew him so well I didn't even need proof to know what he was up to anymore. I had learned to question everything and recognize the small signs that always pointed to something bigger. After several denials from his mother that Adam wasn't there, she finally confessed I was right and that Adam had in fact gone to Jamaica. By the end of our conversation, even Peggy couldn't help agree it was over between us. The same mother whose Jewish instinct had once assured Adam I would reach out to him again, back when he first recovered, finally conceded to our inevitable end. And so did I.

I began writing this memoir in 2008 as a testament of my love for Adam and my willingness to love him unconditionally despite bipolar disorder or any of his other flaws. Perhaps I wanted to be like my mother and love a tainted but worthy man from the depth of my soul. It was never Adam's illness that made him unworthy. It was his unwillingness to bravely rise above it and be a better man. Now, in July 2014, he has moved on and is set to marry another woman. I won't lie. It's taken me some serious time and tears to be able to fully let go. Some days, I'm optimistic, and I imagine he's finally found someone he can be his best self with. Oddly, on those days I'm happy for him. Other days, I pity his future wife, and the inescapable pattern of destruction Adam brings upon those that love him.

I'm not saying those with mental illness can't find true love, or that anyone should not pursue true love with someone who has mental illness.

I'm saying, make sure you know what you're getting into. Don't let the blissful beginning blind you to truths you feel in your gut. Plan a regiment of medication and therapy, together and on your own. Make a commitment and set real expectations at the start of your relationship to work through things together, but promise yourself you'll hold your partner to his or her end of the bargain. Never sacrifice your own sanity and self-worth for anyone. It depletes your value and wastes your time.

I used to pride myself on being someone who lived without regret. That was until I noticed how often I wished I could go back in time and do things differently. When I think about Adam, I can list a hundred things I would've done differently, and my current plan is to do things very differently in my next relationship. But the one thing I'll never regret is the fact that, thanks to Adam, I know what it feels like to truly love another person, to care about something more than I cared for myself. I learned I could survive any situation, no matter how scared or confused I might feel, and persevere, reborn from my ashes, like the Phoenix, permanently scarred into my skin. I learned about mental illness, the severe impact it has on the afflicted, and the lasting effects on those who love them. Loving Adam, I experienced forgiveness and resentment, passion and disdain, ecstasy and pain.

I still hate bugs, though.

A Note on the Fonts

———◆———

This book was set in Hoefler's Requiem, a font inspired
by Ludovico Vicentino degli Arrighi (1480–1527),
a calligrapher at the Apostolic Chancery in Rome and
author of *Il Modo de Temperare le Penne.* The relief font,
Felix Titling—created by the Monotype Drawing Office
in 1934—is based on an alphabet designed by Veronese
calligrapher Felice Feliciano in 1463.

www.ingramcontent.com/pod-product-compliance
Lightning Source LLC
Chambersburg PA
CBHW030825090426

42737CB00009B/884